The Wedge Between Us

By Heidi S. Quimby

Table of Contents

Introduction

Do you have obstacles that are in the way of you becoming all that you want to be? Are you being held back by fears and negative thoughts about who you are and what you are capable of? Do you recognize your self-worth? Have you made mistakes, employed feelings of not being good enough, afraid of being vulnerable, clinging to negative beliefs about yourself or do you just plain lack the confidence to achieve all that is rightfully yours? You are not alone...

Well, since you are still reading, I'm guessing that something has resonated with you right away. If that is the case, then rest assured, you are in exactly the right place at exactly the right time. If you have ever encountered anything that has served as a blocker between you and what you want most out of life, then keep reading. We have all had things get in our way of reaching our goals. I call them, "wedges" and they are crammed into our relationships, forced into our thinking, driven into our belief systems which then create the person we think we are. Wedges are defined as something that is set in place to maintain a gap or separation between two things. They have their place in the world, for things such as splitting wood or plowing a field, however, when they create the space between you and your happiness, they need to be removed.

I have packed this book with stories of challenges, setbacks, and hurdles along with many wedges that have stood between me and my goals. Throughout the pages of my story, you will be inspired to pull out all the stops that are holding you back. I have shared a number of different accounts of my life and how I have learned to become an overcomer! I have had to face adversity many times throughout my life and I expose to you the good, the bad and the ugly in an effort to help you change what is not working for you in your life. I offer you to walk through my journey and apply some of the methods to your own life that have made a tremendous difference in mine.

I wrote this book in hopes to change the life of one person out there who is struggling with hardships that they don't feel as though they can overcome. Having spent much of my life residing in the darkest chambers of my heart, there was little hope for the future. And then something happened that would change the course of my life forever...

The Wedge  Between Us

Chapter 1

The Root of the Problem...

Walking home every day from school was really a drag, especially when it meant that home was the dump on the corner of Acadia and Lisbon Street.

So, the school bus would shoot by loaded with the kids that I went to school with...most of them much wealthier than I. It always seemed to time itself out that I would be just approaching the stairs to our apartment and the bus would be going by simultaneously. I was so ashamed to live in that building of its decrepit condition and pee color that I would keep walking past the entrance and round the corner pretending I lived up the adjacent street.

As a young child, I experienced many occasions in which I felt ashamed or embarrassed. Yeah, the kids at school were not very nice and they teased me about the clothing I wore and my overall "poor" appearance. I wasn't one of the pretty girls but I wasn't the ugliest either, that position was saved for a few select girls like, "Fungus," no kidding, that's what the boys called her.

My fate was maybe a little less than being called a form of mold; however, my mother bought a winter hat for me, which was made by one of the patients at the nursing home where she worked. It read "Hot dog" vertically on both sides and the boys teased that I wasn't hot but I was definitely a dog and commenced to bark at me. It hurt, yes, but I struck back with a tough mug attitude and threatened to start a fight with anyone who would oblige me. Hey, my sister was a couple of grades ahead of me and if I got into trouble over my head, she would rescue me. After all, coming from a family of fighters and the last in line...I had a reputation to protect.

My parents divorced in 1976 when I was only 6 years old. They had a very volatile relationship and were married for about 15 years before splitting. Dad was an alcoholic raised as an only child in a home that didn't foster love and togetherness. I didn't know him that well, and I wasn't his favorite like my older brother and sister, Raymond and Tracy. He would give them a little extra for allowance and tell them not to tell me. He got a kick out of hurting us mentally and physically, like, holding you down until you finally cried and then called you a sissy for not being able to take it. He, along with my mother, would pit us kids against one another. We would fight, like wrestling, with no holds barred and they would egg us on and cheer for one over the other. We all learned to be combative, opinionated, bull headed, stubborn, fighters who wouldn't back down if our lives depended on it. We were "Gauthiers," and we never backed down or said sorry for anything. So the road to hell was being paved and it was never with good intentions.

My mother was argumentative and relentless in staying on my father's ass till he smacked her or beat her down with words – or both. It is something that she should have been used to; possibly it was a comfort to her since that was the way she was raised. Criticism ran rampant in her family of five girls. Mostly prompted by her father...they all learned to critique and pass judgment over others. It was a ritual to go to my grandparents' house in Canton, Maine and sit and listen to everyone fight and bicker until someone cried or nearly had a breakdown trying to prove their point. Seriously, my parents were both immature and had a lot of growing up to do before bringing five children into the world...of course, I am glad that I am here and I thank them for my life and for serving as examples of exactly what not to do. In every household, I think the parents can display one of two things:

1.   What you *should* do...

2. What you *should not* do...

I have decided to take all that knowledge and experience and channel it in a positive direction; I challenge the dominant paradigm and quest to put an end to this cyclical saga.

We had an apartment on Knox Street, which was known as one of the dumpier streets in town. At the tender age of 3 or 4 years old, I haven't much recollection of those days, which is probably a good thing. Times were tough, my parents thoroughly believed that, and so it was. We didn't have much and no one was motivated to try and rise above this way of thinking and make some changes.

Our apartment was dirty, so were our clothes, dishes and just about everything that we owned. Mom was a terrible housekeeper, demotivated and Dad used to bitch at her about it, which never helped, it just made things worse. Besides being dirty, I also remember having rats. Dad caught one in a trap and we all stood around and watched it die, gasping for its breath as it lay there in the trap. What a morbid thing to allow small children to witness as "entertainment" for the evening.

There wasn't a lot to do besides play in the driveway, which we did a lot. When a good rain came, I remember it creating a sort of river along the side of the curb in the street. We would sit in that muddy, filthy water and play for hours. It's a wonder that we never contracted anything from any parasites that I am sure were present in the water. It was usually warm and the current moved swiftly over our little bodies as the water rushed to the drains at the end of the street.

It wasn't all bad memories; we were poor no doubt, but we had some fun times sprinkled in occasionally. Me and my two older sisters, Debbie and Tracy, used to sit in the far corner of a long rectangular closet holding a lamp with no lamp shade, just the stark bulb exposed along with a sleeve of saltine crackers and the tub of butter from the refrigerator. It felt like our secret hideaway and we all bonded in that closet, often.

Another treat was to visit Memere. She lived in the same building, just in the rear. She was the best. She loved us so much. We could get ice cream and other treats when we visited her. She was our Great Grandmother, my father's Grandmother. She always took a shine to my dad...he was a bit of a rebel and she knew it, but she never turned her back to shun him as his own parents did.

Eventually we moved from Knox Street to 938 Lisbon Street, which is where I spent the next 10-12 years of my life. Memere took sick and ended up going into a nursing home with the onset of dementia, known as Alzheimer's today. After moving to Lisbon Street, dad only lived with us for 2 years there.

I remember the fighting, one night in particular where it got bad, real bad. Dad was threatening to choke Mom and Tracy and I were lying on her as protection, crying and refusing to get off of her, as he demanded so that he could choke her. My oldest brother, Ronnie, stood at the door and assured us it would be okay if we got down from her lap, so we did. Dad went after her as he had promised he would and when he did, Ronnie went after him, and we all joined in to protect Mom from getting hurt. The other kids were on him trying to hold him down and I was so stricken with fear that I backed off and stood there fondling my tiny hands, one over the other, crying uncontrollably, not being able to do anything about this. Dad's black-rimmed glasses flew from his face and his Raleigh cigarettes were launched from his shirt pocket, I caught them and was shaking so bad that I squished them until I mutilated the package.

By this time, the police had arrived and they took my father into custody. Through the struggle, he caught his foot between the edge of the braided rug and a piece of furniture in our living room, breaking his leg on the exit out. My mother was screaming such atrocities at him that I can't even repeat some of them. I used to think, "This can't be normal, I wonder if this kind of stuff is going on at my friends' houses. Not!"

After several episodes of being beaten down, Mom kicked him out and filed for a divorce. He moved back "downtown" into a small, one room apartment down the street from his parents. He used to work but became disabled, not sure how, he looked able bodied to me. He was, at the time, unbeknown to me, dying from a fight with emphysema and cirrhosis of the liver. It was truly a battle of which one was going to claim his life first.

For three years, we were allowed to visit him against Mom's better judgment. She never trusted that he would stay sober while we were in his care. We didn't do much when we went to visit him. He took us to visit Memere in the nursing home...this, of course, required us to stop at the Tavern on the corner beforehand, so he could get a beer and a nasty, pickled, green-looking egg from the jar on the counter...gross! He knew how to take the bus there and back and the fee was nominal, 10 cents per person, maybe. From time to time, he made us his infamous spaghetti soup at his apartment, which consisted of water, lard, salt pork, tomato juice and, of course, elbows. It was not anything gourmet but we loved it.

He would also send us to the store one at a time with food stamps to purchase a few pieces of penny candy only to return with the change, which enabled him to buy cigarettes that he couldn't purchase with the stamps. We did it; we were all about the candy!

Usually, it was Tracy and I who visited together, only sometimes did our brother Raymond come with us. One time, I went all by myself. Dad got tired and laid down on the bed. Mom was on her way to come pick me up and so I sat down on the stoop of the doorway leading directly on to the street and waited patiently. He lived on a corner and the apartment used to be an old laundromat.

As I sat there, I watched down the street waiting to see my mother's station wagon pull around to get me. In that time frame, a creepy, suspicious looking man walked by me, making eye contact for a split second. It seemed like quite a few minutes since he had passed me and so I turned my head expecting to see him off in the distance only to find him face to face with me. I was so scared, he grabbed me around my neck and I screamed for my father. Dad got up and stumbled to the door and the man ran away quickly. Mom pulled up and I ran to the car and got inside...it felt safer and I was glad to leave. I'm sorry that I don't remember him being more of a man or a daddy than what he truly was.

Life was hard enough without all the added stress that seemed to accompany me daily. As a child, I was always worried about the bills and how they were going to get paid. My mother vented her frustrations at us, which allowed us to become knowledged and concerned about things that children should not worry about.

The landlady who owned our apartment building would place several calls throughout the month in an effort to collect the rent money, which was always overdue. My mother would wave her hand fiercely signifying that she did not want to talk or even let it be known that she was home...Madame Lachance, (in Mom's French accent) who was as old as dirt, would eventually make an appearance at our house, they would speak in French but much of it I understood, especially the counting, sometimes eight and nine hundred dollars was paid and we still owed more. The landlady was nice but nevertheless she was a businesswoman. She would instruct my mother to pay the rent in full next month and Mom would talk around it and give her just enough to hold her off. I guess that is what she meant by keeping the wolves back away from the door. Mom would be nice to her, of course, while she was at our house, and then when she left and we shut the door she would say, "F*ck you, you money-hungry, old bitch!"

I can't begin to tell you how it feels to be in midstream of washing your hair in the shower and all the lights go off and the water runs cold...the power company shut us down for delinquency on our account. What else is new? I was scared much of the time with a reoccurring thought that, "we are not gonna make it." Much of the struggles that we endured could have been "managed" if the money had been allocated appropriately, but my mother was terrible with money then and she still is today. Unfortunately, that is how the story goes; the children are the ones who suffer at the hands of bad parenting.

I have never been able to understand why neither of my parents never had enough ambition between the two of them to accomplish very much. They simply were not goal-oriented, driven people who sought after achievement in any way. Even after moving from downtown to a nicer apartment, which was still no palace - by the way...my mom still had zero ambition to keep things orderly and maintain us kids. We never discussed goals, what we wanted to be when we grew up, what it takes to achieve or any of the building blocks that create success.

Role modeling for your child is one of the most valuable gifts you can give them. We all know plenty of people who can "tell" you what to do but how many actually "walk that talk", and "show" you how it's done. Lead by example and they will follow and do as you do. Well, it's a good thing I decided to subscribe to another way other than "theirs" or I'd be sitting in the underachievement section of the bleachers of life. Since my early childhood, I have professed to all that I will become more than that of which I came from. The embarrassment, the shame, the ridicule was always more than I could take.

While in grade school, there were multiple occasions where your parents were invited to come in and partake in activities from many different aspects. Most times after a parent-teacher conference, the names of the attending parents remained on the blackboard till the next school day. I was always a little envious to read the names of my classmates' parents. Mr. & Mrs. So & So...my parents were never listed. Parties were coordinated and most mothers helped by bringing in tasteful treats and goodies for the class to enjoy.

I always remembered one mom in particular; she came in often bearing cupcakes or something she had to share. Mrs. Mynahan was her name. She was Timmy's mom, who would go on to pass away from a car accident during his college years. She was an attractive lady with a short, chic, blonde hairstyle that complimented her overall pleasant appearance. She obviously loved her little boy very much and I found myself wishing that she was my mom too! I'm sure she doesn't remember me, even though Timmy and I shared many, if not all, of the same teachers and classes throughout grade school. If I could, I would want her to know that I am grateful for her presence as it allowed me to fantasize of what I thought a mother should look like, smell like, do like and be like. I thank her for that memory.

On an annual basis, parents were invited to come and eat with their child in the cafeteria, in front of all the other kids and their parents. I hated this event and often thought about throwing away the information before my mother could respond.

While she never made it to anything else, she rarely missed this occasion. I was always so ashamed of her ungroomed, unkempt appearance. She was grossly overweight and ate with the zest of a lumberjack, displaying little to no manners at the table. I'm not sure if she was aware of her behavior or if she just disregarded my feelings along with hers because she truly did not know any better or simply did not care. In any event, this was the basis from which I formulated my thinking.

Wow, a lot would have to change if I want my life to be different than what I was raised with. I am destined to be better than what I originated from. I take full responsibility for my life and the things that I have gone through, no blaming, just changing lives in here!

Chapter 2

Angered by Events

My mother was always especially close with her younger sister, Marjorie, even more now that she was away from dad. I think she found solace in the relationship she had with her, after all, my aunt moved away to Connecticut, got out of Canton, Maine, married and had a picture perfect life with 2 children, a boy and a girl, living in a moderate but nice home. We thought they had it all and it was much later that we realized, "all that glittered, wasn't gold." At the time though, we enjoyed spending a few weeks of summer there every year.

In 1979, we were vacationing at my aunt's house in Connecticut when I was nine years old. While innocently playing in the cellar, I was rushing to pick up some balls from a game of pivot pool when my brother appeared at the top of the stairs and screamed down at me frantically, "Dad's dead!"

I think I went into shock, even though I didn't know what shock was back then. The balls I had collected fell through my little hands as my entire body went numb. It was only seconds, but it seemed like slow motion. I scaled those stairs two at a time. I thought my brother was lying; but as I rounded the corner into the kitchen, I saw my mother crying. She was talking long distance to my oldest brother and sister who had stayed behind in Maine. I knew at that moment it was true. Mom rarely cried in front of us kids, so I knew it was really bad. She and dad were divorced, but I could see her pain as she tried to calm my brother and sister and make arrangements to fly home and bury my father.

Not wanting to believe what was happening, I flew out the door and jumped on my cousin's bike. I peddled like never before. On that ride, I remember feeling sensations of sharp knives piercing through my shoulder and chest area. I tried to swallow, but my throat felt like it did the time I got a large piece of a hotdog lodged in it; there was a lump and I couldn't breathe in or out. I remember thinking, "Oh God, my God, no!"

In about ten minutes, I returned to the driveway of my aunt's house and parked the bike in the shed. I went inside and acted like nothing ever happened. I was in denial at that point, and I assured myself that my father was coming back. I didn't understand what death meant or how final it was.

A few years later when I realized that he was not coming back ever, I began to get into trouble at school and with drugs and alcohol. I hated the world and everyone in it. I was especially mad at God. I felt he'd robbed me of things only my father could have taught me. Much later in my life, when the first of my two sons was born in 1990, I began to mature and ask myself some important questions. Was I going to let my father's death continue to eat at me forever? Where was I going in my life, and what kind of mother would I be if I continued to stay angry? I learned from a friend about Christ our Lord. I began to read books and acquire more knowledge. I learned about free will, and that I had the power to turn my scar into a star as many people had done before me.

I have suffered in my life, but so have a lot of other people. I lost my father, but I gained a valuable insight to life that will bear all - the freedom to choose how I will react.

I really didn't understand what death meant or how final it was...Although my relationship was never close with my father, this traumatic event was the catalyst that set into motion many years of anguish which lay ahead waiting for me. It was only the beginning of my life preparing to spiral out of control. Many more undesirable events would take place before I had, as Oprah says, "my light bulb moment or my ah-ha moment."

Not too sure what my mother had to gain by telling me that my father never liked me, but she made it known that I was not his favorite by any stretch. There would be many more times to come in which she ignored my feelings and how certain choices would impact me. She would share information with me and the others that was simply destructive. After he passed away, there would never be any good that would come from this knowledge, especially when he wasn't here to inquire of the alleged nor was he here to defend it.

It all began from the day I was born. For whatever reason, she chose me to be her favored one. This caused nothing but trouble for me beginning with my earliest of recollect and continuing right to present date. When I was a small child, her partiality was one sort of monster that began to separate me from the rest of the kids.

From time to time, we would catch hell for doing things that Mom didn't approve of. I remember being the "out" for those who displayed bad behavior. The older kids would say, "Tell Mom that Heidi did it!" or "She won't come down on her that hard, she's mom's pet and will not get punished severely, like us, probably not even at all." Little did I know that this would be the beginning of the wars between my four older siblings and me.

When you are a parent of more than one child, you must be careful and creative in keeping things even. If you dote, favor or cater to one more than the other(s), this will almost assuredly create disharmony. For the child who is not the favored one, they will almost, with certainty, become resentful of the sibling who gets his/her way and enjoys special rights and privileges. They not only become resentful, but often times, never learn how to become a person with high self-esteem yielding a positive self-image. This child will always have the feelings of inadequacy, since they were not "good enough" to receive any special treatment. They go on feeling defective and insufficient in many areas of their lives.

In my family, it has always been Them against Me. The segregation that has been encouraged by my mother's hand has literally driven a wedge between us children. Like a wood splitter, the wedge was set in place, the blow from the mallet was delivered and we are the pieces that have fallen to the ground. It may not have been so obvious to me as a young girl but the picture becomes clearer as the pieces begin to fit back together.

In my tender years, it was more about the older children complaining that, "Mom never let me stay up till 9:00pm on a school night, boy, times have changed or at least the rules have!" or "I never got any new clothes, I always wore hand-me-downs!" For me, this created a feeling of guilt that I have things or can do things and they don't or can't. I always tried not to stand out too much since any previous feelings of guilt would have me feeling like I should be suffering or going without too.

This is the character of the martyr who lives within me. It has led me to my own demise on several occasions. I have more than likely, sabotaged my own success over the years, with the idea, "I shouldn't have this. Other people don't have it, so...What makes me so special?" It has been troubling, to say the least, to overcome many of these notions that were planted in my head as a child. I would have liked to believe that any person being in an authoritative position would steer you in all the most positive directions for an optimum result. Be careful whose words you allow to shape your perspective for unfortunately, they may not have your best interest at heart.

Looking at a snapshot into the future, I did arrive at the point where I had to take a long look in the mirror and identify the aspects of my life that I considered to be undesirable. I would not be who or where I am today if I was not willing to take that first step. All the while that I was educating myself across the various facets of my life, I reiterated the information to anyone who would listen. I was captivated by the things I was learning and couldn't wait to share them. I began to implement them into my life, which yielded change in a positive direction. I had to internalize these concepts and prepare myself for change.

The best plans in the world are not going to lead you to success if you fail to execute them. I think that is where a lot of people stop short. Knowledge and information is everywhere around you but if there is no follow through, no implementation of any of the strategies learned, it's like riding a stationary bike and getting nowhere fast.

My mother is full of great advice and know-how, but fails to practice any of what she preaches. The best decision I ever made was to stop listening to her and start listening to me. At this stage in my life, I was in the best position to decide what is right for me, no one else. But, before I would get to the "epiphany mode"...I would have to take a few more tests before I understood the lessons to be learned. In school, we would have traditionally gotten the lessons first and then tested of our knowledge later. In God's world, you are tested first and revealed the lesson later. Similar to staying back a grade is the one clause that goes like this...*if you do not receive the lesson as instructed to learn, you must repeat the test, over and over if needed until you meet the requirement to move on to the next life lesson.* Yeah, I'm a little stubborn but I'm far from stupid, things get a little hairier before it all begins to come together, read on...

Chapter 3

Testimonials -

I do have a Guardian Angel

I believe everything happens for a reason. Many things have happened to me in my life that I cannot explain. We are all given one life to live; and at times, I feel as though I used that one and nine more to boot. I must have a greater purpose here on Earth that only God knows about. He has forgiven me over and over again, for so many of my unfaithful times. On several different accounts, God has placed people in my path at the exact time when I needed to be rescued. It was never by coincidence but only a GODcidence that my life has been spared.

As a young girl, one of my earliest recollections was being saved by my mother in a near drowning episode. We used to live and die for 3 o'clock to roll around with the anticipation of going to Sabbathday Lake, which was about thirty minutes from our house. Mom would pack boloney and cheese sandwiches with mustard (gross!) and using an empty milk container, she would rinse it out and mix up a jug of Kool-Aid along with some paper cups. We couldn't afford to eat out for heaven sakes; but once in a while, we did stop at the Custard's Last Stand for a frozen yogurt, small sizes of course. We went to this lake several times and I was never allowed to swim out to the raft. This time was no different except my two older siblings were strong enough swimmers to make the swim out. I was told to stay back.

I swam back and forth parallel to the beach until I felt comfortable enough to holler out to my Mom and tell her I think I can do it. She was hesitant, but I insisted and so she waved her arm, giving me the ok. While I was swimming in the more shallow water, I could see all the way to the bottom, but as I began to charter deeper waters, everything below me turned black. I found myself in a state of panic and began gulping water and going under. I flailed my arms and legs in an effort to keep my head above water but I was scared to the point of paralysis.

Every time my head would make it past the surface, I could see them on the raft. The last time I remember seeing anything was mother standing on the edge of the raft and even though she was several yards away from me I could see her panic-stricken face as I had never seen that look in her eyes before. I recall seeing her do this fantastic swan dive off that raft and how she fought to swim to me with her nosepiece on and no strength to make it on her own.

Thank God that her friend, Pauline, was in the water and saw what was happening and began swimming out to me. When my mother reached me, she had nothing left in the tank, she passed me off to Pauline and they got me to the shore. I had never been so paralyzed with fear before that day. I could see myself going under and I didn't think I was going to make it. God had another plan for me, he gave my mother the strength she needed to get to me...He saved me then and in so many ways since then and I didn't even realize His greatness until much later.

Another disturbing testimonial that involved water was an episode that happened to me while visiting a racquetball club with my childhood best friend, Tina. Her mom agreed to bring us girls with her so long as we stayed in the spa area and didn't pester her while she was playing in the courts. We were around 12 years old and not sufficient age to play racquetball; it was the club's policy. We didn't care about playing ball anyway; we just liked using the Jacuzzi. We got to the spa and her mom laid down the rules and we agreed to behave.

After she left, we changed into our swimsuits and slid the glass doors open and entered into the tub area. We talked and relaxed for a bit and then decided that we would see who could stand to put their face under the hot water the longest. So, we each did it a couple of times and we were having fun with it. Then when it was my turn, I sunk down the wall on my back and submerged my head under water and in the blink of an eye, all my hair was sucked into a return drain leaving my face and mouth about four inches beneath the water and away from my next breath. I could see the lights on the ceiling casting sort of a shimmery, sunburst through the water that rippled and whirled over the top of my body. I began to perceive the depth in which my only air source was being quantified as out of reach from my mouth.

I struggled to free myself for what seemed like forever and I began to panic and thought...this is my end. I was thinking a lot of things, why wasn't Tina helping me? She was so distraught watching me thrash and roll around trying to free myself that she couldn't move. I was pulling and tugging and squirming and wiggling around as I was nearing the last of the air I had in me. Just when I was ready to give up, my last tug was a mighty one...and it was as though someone hit a release valve or something, and I wasn't trapped anymore. I gasped for air and began to bawl when I had enough breath to do so. I still did not recognize that I was on the receiving end of God's merciful hand!

I went on to race around in cars while high on cocaine, riding on the back of motorcycles with the daredevils who liked pulling wheelies till my head was barely an inch above the ground. Traveling at speeds that would have killed me instantly if we had laid that bike down, not to mention, uhm, no helmet! So, what is my purpose? Throughout my life, I have never been truly clear on what the heck I am supposed to do, or rather "who" I am supposed to be. I have been a daughter, mother, sister, aunt, friend, wife and many more titles that I thought revealed my purpose for being here. I have come to realize that those descriptions are "what" I am to others but they don't come close to defining "who" I am and what I will accomplish while I'm here on Earth.

I have awakened to the reality that my purpose is defined by my ability to serve others. Throughout my lifetime, God has used me to help those in need. He shows me what I need to see and then internally nudges me to take action and avail myself to those who require assistance. I am moved by His Spirit. He is the reason that I write these words. If I can help one other person to rehabilitate their life and incorporate meaning and purpose to their very existence, I have served them and my Lord well.

When I moved to 938 Lisbon Street...my oldest brother, Ronnie, was friends with a boy named Gary. He took me with him over to Gary's house to play with Gary's kid sister, Tina, while they played pass. She was about six months older than me but at the tender age of four, it didn't matter much. She was shy and I wasn't sure how to approach her and then we shared a flower and she asked me to be her friend and play. We hit it off as best friends and we were inseparable for years to come. I spent many days and nights over at Tina's house, so much that it felt like I had become part of their family. I ate dinner there lots of nights, slept over, cleaned and helped with dishes.

To me, her parents were the ideal parents. They had a perfect middle class family dynamic much like that of the Cunninghams on the hit TV series, *Happy Days*. Although they were the Charests, they became known as Mr. & Mrs. C to me. They were a good Catholic family who ate together, went to church together, vacationed together; they had everything in a family that I wanted. They looked after me and accepted me into their home many times, probably when they were really wishing that I would just go home to my own house. My mother and Tina's mother were friendly which now leads me to understanding that Mrs. C may have known more of what was going on with me in my home life. She opened her heart to me.

She really was like a second mother to me. I am thankful to them both for having a hand extended when I needed it the most. For the most part, Tina and I got along like two peas in a pod. Oh yeah, we were totally inseparable as kids. Whatever trouble two girls could get into, we did. We went everywhere together and spent all of our summers with each other. One of our favorite things to do was to play jokes. The two of us had some good times. We had our share of fights and disagreements, but when we pulled pranks, we meshed together like peanut butter and jelly, the perfect match.

Andy's was the local convenience store down the road from Tina's house. She would call them up first, asking them if they had pig's feet. When they replied yes, she would say, "You must look pretty funny in sandals!" Then it was my turn. I called up and asked if they had Prince Albert in a can. When they left the telephone to check the aisle, I would laugh hysterically. I knew that I was going to tell them to let him out because his mother wanted him home for supper. While taking turns, we each came up with something funnier than the time before.

We always made sure that we disguised our voices too. After all, we were faithful customers who spent any available funds we could get our hands on in the game room there every Saturday afternoon. We did not want them on to us.

Another one of our most infamous pranks to play was calling taxicabs and sending them to neighbors that we hated. We would call up Two-in-One taxi service and send them to Jenny Page's house. She was an ugly, little, redhead that lived up the road. She was always coming around bugging to play with us. Since Jenny was two whole grades under us, we were not about to be seen with the likes of her. We would sit in the picture window of Tina's living room and watch the cab pull up to her house and blow its horn. Laughing uncontrollably, we saw her mother come out in her housecoat to find out why the car was waiting and beeping out there. She was so hideous with curlers in her hair. What a guff!

We played another one of our tricks on a snotty couple who lived down the street. We always hated them because they hated all kids, including us. I wonder how they liked it when we sent twenty loaded pizzas to their house that day we were bored. We were probably the reason that stores started taking your name and number for large orders. What a gas! We were brats, but we sure had a lot of fun.

Looking back, we did have many laughs. We played these jokes daily, all summer long. They might not have been very nice, but at least nobody got hurt. Those were some of the best of times. I wish I could be little again, even if it was only for just one day.

Along with the good, the bad always accompanied in some way, shape or form. Well, Tina and I were certainly not saints...in fact we had been experimenting with a little cigarette smoking with my older sister, Tracy. It was lucky for me that Tracy liked Tina and didn't mind her accompanying us most anywhere we went.

My sister and I shared a paper route; we distributed about 110 papers daily. She was not only older than me but also bigger and stronger and therefore shouldered around 85 papers compared to my measly 25. I had to do Lisbon Street though and that meant a lot of crossing back and forth over the busiest street in Lewiston.

Tracy did the side streets, which connected at one end by a small trail. We always made it a weekly ritual to go out to eat at Bonanza before doing our route. We would collect for the weekly paper, put away the amount we needed to pay the bill and then split the profit. Well, sometimes, we spent a little of the profit first and then stressed to collect the rest to make the bill when it was due. This particular day, we spent a little up front. We enjoyed a package of cigarettes and then a nice meal at the restaurant.

On the walk home, Tracy was mad at me. She kept calling me a little bitch since Tina was going with me on my half of the route and not her. She hardly thought I needed help to distribute my 25 papers and reasoned that Tina should go with her since she had more of the route than me. I wouldn't hear of it and we squabbled; but in the end, Tina came with me. It was also the 17th of February and cold outside and that just added to her frustration. It was three days past my birthday. She just wouldn't cut me any slack and wouldn't stop being mean to me.

We all three arrived at our house; we ran upstairs to grab our route bags and get busy on our afternoon duty. I didn't know what was taking Tracy so long but Tina and I were ready, so we left. We got downstairs and to the side of the busy street. It had been snowing all afternoon but was beginning to accumulate now and coming down much harder. We crossed out to the center over one lane of traffic and were stuck waiting in the middle of the road. The tension grew as we stood there hand-in-hand, Tina in her long, green, fluffy coat and I with my down vest which held the cigarettes we purchased earlier in an inside pocket.

At that moment, Tina made the decision to take one step back and I made the decision to go forward. In a split second, we unlocked and let go of each other's hands. For me, everything went into slow motion picture takes. I assessed how far the car was from me and how quickly it was moving and thought I had enough time to make it to the other side. As the car drew nearer, everything was in slow motion and the car moved in picture takes like the way they used to show films, page by page, back before the days of editing, splicing and technological advancements took place.

Time stood still for me at that moment and the car struck me in the legs and threw me up onto the top roof and I dropped down the side of the driver's door snagging my face on the door handle. While flipping through the air, I did not feel anything...I didn't know what had happened to me.

At the onset of the slow motion realm, I entered into a tunnel with pictures on the walls all around me. It was like little TV screens plastered all over every square inch of this tunnel playing the events of everything that had ever happened to me throughout my entire lifetime. I stood with my family and friends at my back but not far behind me, and a bright white light with robed figures waited at the other end. They appeared to be much farther away than my family and friends, who were closer behind me. The figures were silent in volume but were telling me that it was okay to come forward and I would be safe. My family and friends were screaming in high volumes not to go forward. "Turn around," they said, and "Come back!"

I felt like this was a decision for me to make all by myself. I chose to turn away from the inviting light and remain with my family and friends. When I came to, I was running in the street. In a sense, I knew I had landed in the other lane of traffic and was not safe. I somehow knew enough to fall down, hit the ground and get up and head for the side of the road for my safety. I have been told that I never made it to the side before I dropped in the street.

A woman who lived up the road from me and who also was a route carrier helped me without hesitation. Her name was Mrs. Chabot. She didn't know me and I didn't really know her. She truly was an angel. I could see her through the blurred vision I was experiencing at this point, moving to get out of the street, my face full of blood from the gash on the side of my head. I could see her coming at me and she took me and guided me to the side of the street and safe out of harm's way from getting hit over and over. I thank her for having a kind spirit and helping me that day.

The old man, who sold bicycles on the opposite corner where I lived, ran out and put his smelly old jacket on me. Bless his heart for caring. Before I knew it, someone had been to the call box and rang for every branch of assistance that was offered. Police, fire trucks and ambulance filled the street.

My older brother, Raymond, appeared over me asking me if I knew my name...I did. He had phoned my mother at the club downtown to let her know of the incident. He quickly relayed over the phone, "Mom, Heidi's been hit by a car, come home quick!"

In no condition to drive, she was chauffeured home by a friend to come upon a scene like out of the movies. Sirens and lights filled the air as she drove up on all the chaos. She quickly learned that I was okay and entered into the ambulance crying, looking to hold me and tell me that everything was gonna be okay. Still worried that the package of smokes would be found on me, they took my coat off but when I got it back, there they were safe and sound and she never found out.

I was physically evaluated to find that I only had a reddened area on my leg that would eventually turn into a black and blue spot over the next several days. The gash on my head was minimal after the blood was clotted and cleaned. Often times, head wounds bleed profusely; and when cleaned up, they appear to be not much more than a scrape. I was very lucky and have thanked God many times since then for sparing my life that day.

When I arrived home, I learned that my friend, Tina, was pretty shakened up...she would not calm down until she spoke to me directly. I called her and assured her that I was okay and would be back to normal by morning. And I was. As I flip through the pages of my life, I realize that this was one of many in which my life would be spared. God had a greater plan for me; I just didn't know it yet.

Tracy apologized to me many times for being mean to me that day. We grew closer together from that experience, I think. She may have wanted to kill me in the past since I was a pest to her in many ways; but in the end, she realized she never wanted anything really bad to happen to me. She became even more and more giving over the next several years. She always "looked out" for me; she was always good to me like that.

I was still very bitter from my father's death and didn't quite see clearly any of the good that was around me. I was a bit of a rebel; and at the time, it felt like I had cheated death and lived to tell about it.

Chapter 4

Growing Up – "Gauthier" Style

What else could I get myself involved in that would lead me to self-destruct? That seemed to be the path I was travelling, one of condemnation. I didn't care. I had a lousy attitude and just didn't give a damn about anything or anyone, including myself.

So, my path of self-sabotage did not end for a long period of time and many more mishaps would take place before it would be done. Not only was I smoking cigarettes now on a regular basis, I had my own pack upon entering seventh grade.

I began to smoke marijuana with my friends but mostly with my oldest brother, Ronnie and my sister, Tracy. We would go down to Ron and his wife, Kathy's house and get high all the time. I babysat my niece and my brother paid me with pot.

Higher than a kite, my niece, Kalene, was just a baby and left in my care. I watched over her, I guess. She cried a lot; and most of the time, Julie, my other best friend, would accompany me. She could always console Kalene and get her to go to sleep, which was quite a feat.

Julie and I went on to continue smoking dope with anyone who would light up with us. We had known each other since kindergarten but never hung out much until we reached junior high school. Her mother, Judy, used to walk all the neighborhood kids to school; she was a stay-at-home mom and was always available.

Her dad, Charlie, worked at Crest Shoe with my dad back in the day. He would tell me of the very few recollections he had of my dad, but it was sometimes consoling just to know that he knew him. In a way, it was a connection to him that I didn't have with many others. I yearned for that, a way to stay attached to him. I guess that meant that I never had to let him go.

By the time I was entering my teenage years, my life really began to spiral out of control. From one thing to another, I was in trouble for something. I grew this amazingly huge chip on my shoulder and was looking for someone to challenge me and try....just try to knock it off, always upholding the "Gauthier" mantra!

I never really had much of a male role model in my life. After my father passed away, my mother had a couple of boyfriends that came and went. When I turned 10 years old, she had taken up with a guy named Roland from downtown in her club scene. He began living with us and things seemed to get a little better on the home front at least at first. Roland was a simple man, not very educated to the degree where he argued with us kids as though he was a child himself. He worked for a moving company and was very strong in the physical sense; however, he was also an alcoholic and had been one for years. When he began living with us, the housework began to get done. He had a few strikes against him in some areas, but he knew how to take care of our basic needs. Roland did the dishes, sometimes 2 or 3 times a day, unlike the months' worth that sat there day in and day out prior to his arrival.

I can remember wanting to have a bowl of cereal and never having a clean bowl or silverware to do so. It was maddening that every time you wanted something to eat you would have to hunt through the stacks of dirty dishes to find the appropriate dish for your need, and wash it for a single use. I would reach down in the basin that sat in the sink, left by someone who had prepared to do the dishes but never got any farther; attempting to retrieve a spoon from the water which was gray in color and cold from the drafty window above the sink. I used to think, "Why do we have to live like this? This isn't the way it's supposed to be."

Laundry was the same; the clothes had been shoved down in the hamper in the bathroom so hard that the wicker container had sprouted a hole at the bottom and the clothes had now spilled out onto the floor. When that hamper got sorted finally after months, I would find clothing that I hadn't worn for six months. It almost felt like Christmas and I was getting a little something new to wear.

Roland changed a lot of that when he entered our family. I now had clean clothes to wear and clean dishes to eat from. He picked up the house incessantly and made it a better environment for all of us. Our apartment was still a dump but it was a cleaner dump thanks to Roland. His work was not steady and neither was the paycheck.

After a few years, it became less and less and mom and him fought more and more. Mom's intelligence level was far superior to his and she welcomed the opportunity to beat him at a battle of wits. He eventually became more like a boarder than her lover. I didn't really care what was going on between them emotionally. All I knew was that our standard of living was a little better when he entered the scene. He took care of me and I loved him a lot.

Up until this point in his life, all he really had was his dog, Shirley. She was an added plus when Roland came to live with us. We always hounded mom for a dog, no pun intended, and she always said, "No way." Roland and Shirley were a package deal and he wouldn't have come to live with us if he couldn't bring her. That dog meant the world to him. When they fought, he would tell

Mom to go take care of "her" kids and she would respond, go take care of "your" dog. I guess fair was fair; they each felt a share of ownership over what was "theirs" while the other had no say when it came to decisions made in "our" best interest or the "dog's" best interest.

I hated being stuck in that apartment throughout the week and especially on the weekends. The oldest of us five kids was Ronnie, and he had had a falling out with Roland shortly after his arrival to live with us. Roland got into it with Ronnie one night; and through the scuffle, mom kicked Ron out of the house. He left that night and never came back to live with us again.

Next in age was Debbie, just a year younger than Ronnie, she had decided to strike out on her own even before Roland came to our house. She and Mom could never see eye to eye. Debbie had aspirations to look like somebody in spite of where she came from. She was a beautiful girl and Mom was always jealous of the sense of pride she took in herself. She labeled her as being "self-absorbed." She basically was never there as a mother for Debbie and drove her out to go elsewhere to make a life for herself.

So, now it was down to the three youngest, Raymond, Tracy and I. We seemed like the second generation anyway, since there was a four-year gap between Debbie and Raymond and eight years between Debbie and I with Tracy falling in between us.

Through some of our younger years, Raymond and I were closer in the sense that we both were early risers in the morning. We enjoyed playing kickball in the living room, marbles on the braided carpet, around the world with the nerf ball or just watching cartoons. Of course, we loved to fight as well. On the weekends, it was nothing for us to make 3, 4, even 5 phone calls per day to the nursing home looking for mom to play mediator in our squabbles. She would get so mad when we bothered her at work for what she considered "foolishness."

She always left us strict instructions in the morning with a lineup of tasks for each one of us. It was always conveyed through a note that was found lying on the table. It would usually read what tasks were to be completed by who and lots of underlying, exclamation points and most assuredly closed with "OR ELSE" in caps, which you knew meant business. We never actually questioned or found out what "OR ELSE" meant; you just knew not to disobey or there would be hell to pay later.

Mom was not one to speak at you two and three times to get you to respond. When she spoke once, you knew you had better move. She wasn't exactly a small woman in stature. Weighing in at

200+lbs, coupled with a fierce backhand, she was a force not to be reckoned with. She had a very low tolerance for us most of the time anyway, so when she was angered, it was not the time to push her buttons. Sometimes it felt as though she resented having us. With Dad gone, she was left all alone, holding the bag.

Tracy always awakened later than Raymond and I. We all were not much for conversation with one another unless it meant arguing and fighting. Raymond really didn't like Tracy and me much at all back then. At school, we served as an embarrassment to him and he wanted no association with us whatsoever. I suppose he had his own demons that he was dealing with in his own way.

Tracy and I, on the other hand, were very close. We were different in that she was a slob in our shared room, while I remained neat and tidy. We were like Oscar and Felix from the show, *The Odd Couple*. She was, of course, Oscar, and I was Felix. I was small and skinny and she was always a little bigger and fatter. She had to wear Huskys and Toughskins from Sears, since none of the hand-me-downs from our cousin, Denise, would fit her.

I was fortunate that when a bag of clothes was sent up from my Aunt Marge in Connecticut...it was all nice stuff, laundered and well folded, ready for me to wear right out of the bag. The problem came when I wore things once; I never saw them again for months. Growing up at 938 Lisbon Street wasn't anything to write home about, that's for sure. So, life goes on and more experiences and learning curves would lie ahead.

By my teenage years, I had given up on most of everything. Nothing really mattered to me anymore. Home life was getting worse and I just could not connect with my mother. I think it must have been the beginning of the resentment that I still feel today. I could never do anything right or good enough; she was never proud of me for anything. She reminded me constantly how the things that came out of my mouth were so stupid, and that travelling the road that I was on, I wasn't going very far. This type of abuse towards me just reinforced an already low self-esteem and negative self-image. Day in and day out, life was just stinky at 938 Lisbon Street.

As kids, we spent an awful lot of time at home, alone! We had each other, yeah, to fight with. Mom worked 7am-3pm every day and we fought from sun up to sun down. Always waiting on her to get home from work, just to find out that she's sitting down at the club having a diet Pepsi, wasting her life and ours too! Yes, she was only drinking diet soda, not booze, but we still felt her absence. She was disgruntled as if she *was* a pissed off alcoholic.

The only thing worse, was when we were en route to someplace and she needed to sign her weekly pool in hopes to win it big. We would have to stay in the car and wait for her. Sometimes she forgot that we existed; she sat in there like she was a single woman, no kids and on a vacation or something.

She always seemed to be angry with us for some reason. One of us was always in trouble for something. I can remember a time, when as a teenager, she had grounded me or didn't allow me to go out to something I had planned and I mumbled, under my breath, that she was being a "bitch." Of course, she heard it and came stomping down the hall after me as I fled into my bedroom. I didn't get the door closed behind me and she was there with her hand on it preventing me from my escape. It startled me and I knew I was going to get it now!

When she got angry, we all feared for our lives. She entered my room and stared me straight in the eyes with every ounce of hatred; she began to slap me in the head and across my face. She was over the top of me as I lay across the bed on my back, trying to cover up from the blows she was delivering. I eventually gave up trying to block her from connecting with my face and she commenced to hitting me several times over and over. While I was down, I thought, "If I just let her get the good swipes in that she's looking for, she will stop and this will end."

After counting five and six slaps, I realized she wasn't stopping and many more followed. I remember thinking, "Okay, this is outta control. She is losing it and she's gonna really hurt me." When the hitting stopped, it was because my jaw had been about broken and was sticking to the side in the direction she was slapping it in. I was so scared! Something snapped in her when she hit us and it wasn't normal. She had a lot of pent up anger and issues that should have been counseled. I really did feel like she was going to kill me or something.

When she finally left me alone and returned to the living room, I made a break for it. She thought, since we lived in an apartment on the second floor, that I was stuck and couldn't leave. I opened the window and looked down upon the roof of the Silhouette Beauty Salon, crawled out and jumped about ten feet onto the roof and ran to the end of the building for another six-foot drop to my freedom. There was a narrow alley that separated our apartment building from the beauty salon. People partied in there, broke glass, vomited, urinated and all sorts of nasty things. I never once worried about not clearing that mess to make the jump to the roof, like a trapped animal, when I wanted out. I was willing to do whatever it took to get away from her. After that episode, amongst many others, I never trusted my mother again and our relationship changed forever.

Chapter 5

The Calm before the Storm

By my freshman year of high school, I was making some bad choices for myself that would come back to bite me later. Twelve days into the school year, I decided to hand in my drop out papers. I was at the school to do just that when I saw a friend of mine standing there, talking with another guy I was interested in meeting.

There he stood in his tight, faded Levi's, the cutest boy in school, talking to someone I knew. Here was my chance to introduce myself. I approached them with confidence "Hey!" I said, "I'm Heidi. Who are you?" (Like I didn't already know.)

He turned his face my way. His features were dark and perfect. He sported a thin mustache and lengthy brown hair that lay limp upon his worn jean jacket. He began to speak with a raspy, tough voice and said, "I'm Richie." My hands grew sweaty as I stood there. In the distance, I could hear the sounds of hydraulics squeezing air as the door to the school busses opened which ended the day. The clanging of chains freed the bicycles from their racks. In the bustle, I could hear parents holler their children's names and beep their horns to get their attention. Bodies filled the cold stone wall as kids made their plans for the weekend. As we stood there, I waited for him to say something, anything.

He offered to take me for a ride on his motorcycle. I accepted and sprung onto the back as if I had been catapulted. I wrapped my arms around his waist and "eek"ed inside with excitement. He turned the key and the motor purred with a slight flutter.

The seat was stiff and uncomfortable, but I didn't care. He snapped a pedal from down below with the toe of his boot, and before I knew it, we were mobile. I peered into the mirrors, which gave me a straight view of him. We both looked funny as the wind whipped our hair back and the skin on our faces rippled over our cheeks. He kept a stern, poised look on his face. With a pair of Oakley sunglasses on, he almost looked like Fonzie from the television series *Happy Days*.

Nightfall was approaching as the sun began to disappear behind the buildings. I had to go home, but I wished this day didn't have to end. Richie drove me to my house and I hesitantly dismounted the bike. We stood there and were distracted a moment by the buzzing of the outside lamppost as the halogen light began to illuminate the driveway. I waited expectantly for him to kiss me. As he came closer, I could smell the sweet fragrance of his cologne blending with the tic-tac he had just popped in his mouth. He leaned forward and pressed his warm lips against mine. For a moment, I felt like I was going to melt.

After we kissed, I was so nervous I just turned around and began walking up the way. Feeling as if I had eyes watching me, moving with my every step, I turned around and asked, "Will I see you again?" He replied, "You bet!" I watched him leave that night and never expected that I would not only marry him but also endure the living hell that I would later identify as my life.

By January, my mother had really just gotten to her wit's end with me and it was decided that she would ship me down to live with my strict Aunt and Uncle in Connecticut. I went to live there in January and things were okay for a while. I got registered for school, shots and the whole nine yards.

I began working at the Ramada Inn where my Aunt was employed. I was a chambermaid, nothing glorious, but I felt a sense of accomplishment that I hadn't felt for a very long time, if ever. I met a guy named Johnny shortly after I arrived. I had many friends within a short period of time.

My oldest cousin, Pudge, whose room I was occupying, was gone off to the Air Force and my other cousin, Denise, was a year ahead of me in school. We were extremely close as kids growing up but we weren't really that close while I lived with her and her family. We had certainly evolved into two very different people.

After spending about 5 months there, I decided that I'd had enough. One day, while sitting in Mr. Kausche's science class, I asked to use the bathroom, went to my locker, grabbed a couple of personal things and bummed a ride from a couple of seniors in the parking lot. They took me to the highway. I got out, waved good-bye and started on my way back to Maine.

I hadn't done a whole lot of thumbing up to this point but became very good at it. It wasn't long before I reached Lewiston and my mother quickly learned of my return. I tried to go back and live with her over the summer but it just wasn't working for me. That whole summer, I spent time going back and forth from Maine to Connecticut...just to visit for the day. I did have to return to get my things. I had clothes, personals, record albums, stuffed animals, jewelry box...everything that a 15-year-old girl would have in their room, minus any furniture.

On the trip down to get my things, my friend, Shelene, accompanied me. She was one of my many partners in crime. We made it down just fine, got plenty of rides and no weirdos. When we got there, we began walking down the street close to my Aunt's house. My cousin Denise and her boyfriend drove by and saw us. She convinced me to get in the car and assured me that her mother was not angry with me; she was just concerned of my well-being. Of course, she was lying to me. Reluctantly, as if I knew it was a trap, I got in.

When I met up with my aunt, she was anything but nice. She called my mother and informed her of my arrival. Unbeknownst to me at the time, I had been reported to authorities weeks ago and listed as a runaway. My aunt then took us to the police station and turned us in.

After speaking with us briefly, they gave us two options: we could either spend the night there in jail or be relinquished into the custody of my aunt until the morning. We opted to go to my aunt's house. As I weighed my options, I figured, my aunt's house versus jail...hmmm, same thing, basically, except all my stuff was at my aunt's house and I had to go there and get it anyway.

Shelene and I loaded my things into large garbage bags and placed them into the car. My aunt was going to drive us to the bank where I could withdraw the only money I had, 140 bucks.

It wasn't from her kind heart that she offered the ride, it was only that I owed her $25 dollars and she wanted to collect that from me before I left town. After paying her the money I owed her, she let us unload my bags from the car and left us both standing there in the bank parking lot without so much as a good bye. She could be a very kind and giving person, but she could also be mean and cruel with her words and actions, which left you wondering does she even have a heart?

With everything I had in me, we lugged all my stuff to the edge of the Ella Grasso Turnpike in hopes to get a ride back home to Maine. I had so many bags that we tried to keep moving as we were thumbing but it was taking two and three trips to move only a short distance. We shortly figured out that this was not going to work.

Many vehicles passed us by since they just didn't have the room for all of my trumpery. Finally, a guy with a flatbed pickup truck stopped and helped us load everything on and he took us to the Massachusetts Turnpike. We were so grateful but still had a long road ahead of us to Lewiston, Maine. We stood and sat and laid down with all of that stuff, hitching for a ride that seemed would never come.

A truck driver stopped and I went to the door. I opened it up and he asked, "Where you headed?" I said, "Lewiston, Maine." He replied, "I'm going to Portland, jump in!" We couldn't get in there fast enough, what a lucky break! Portland was only about 45 minutes South of Lewiston.

We were well on our way home and I felt a bit spiteful to those I held responsible for my unfortunate situation. Never blamed my own bad decision-making process, just looked to blame someone other than me. Ha, they thought I would cower down and resort to calling them for help, NEVER!! I was a "Gauthier," remember, and I don't back down to anything, EVER!

Some of that mindset is probably what got me through many of the difficult challenges I have faced. I have always been reluctant to quit anything, even when it's not a good thing for me anymore. It is very clear to me now, of course, that my ability to discern between right and wrong and good and bad was certainly distorted.

So, the first trucker got us as far as he was going and we did end up getting another ride the rest of the way from Portland to Lewiston, only it was about midnight at this point. Shelene and I were considered to be runaways and we didn't want to be spotted by anyone. The night was a great cover until I realized that along the ride home, Shelene had taken sick, real bad. We went to a friend's house where we had to call her mother and she was going back home, which left me solo again. I remained on the run for a while but my funds were running out and I eventually called my Mom. She wanted me to come home and I did. The cycle began all over again.

I ended up moving in with a family who lived on the next street over from me. The Tolinis. They were a nice family who agreed to let me live with them while I tried to get my life in order.

Their daughter, Denise, and I were good friends; she was a senior in high school, while I was a freshman. I tried to go back to school while I was living with them but most of the time skipped to get high.

I had reconnected with that guy, Richie that I wanted to meet when I was at the high school turning in my drop out papers at the beginning of the school year. He and Denise were friends. In fact, he was friends with everyone and had gained much popularity and notoriety as being the biggest pot dealer in the history of Lewiston High School. He was a rebel, had a lot of friends from dealing, always came equipped with a bag of dope and I found him to be a person of interest.

Shortly into our school year, Denise decided to move to a neighboring town, Auburn, with her boyfriend and I went along too. The agreement was that she and Dave would pay the rent for the first month and then I would be responsible for the next month and we would switch off every other month.

I had to get a job and decided that waitressing would yield me the most income. In spite of being underage, at fifteen, I lied on my application and got a job up the hill from our apartment at the local Denny's restaurant. I started as a hostess that earned me about $73/week and my rent was $75/week. I was already in the hole for two bucks and hadn't even eaten yet.

Times were certainly tough and I was learning firsthand what it felt like to be hungry. There were times that I lay on the floor and cried because I was so hungry. I was just a kid and strapped with a lot of adult issues. Seemed like par for the course since this had been the way of life in which I grew up.

I used to worry about the bills as a child, especially since the power at home was once turned off when I was in the middle of a shower. As I stated before, we never paid our rent in full and there was never enough food to last the entire month. Yeah, we got food stamps and all, but Mom spent all of it at the beginning of the month, we ate like kings for the first week or so, then there was nothing left. I was hungry then too, but not like I was living in my own place, trying to play grown up.

I did get more hours at work when I moved from hostess to waitress. Policy was that if you worked a shift of four consecutive hours, you were entitled to a meal. My ship had come in; one meal a day was better than no meals for several days.

Still, I reached some all-time lows while I lived there. I slept on a spring filled, dumpy hide-a-bed in the living room that doubled as our couch.

There were no extras and I found this out quickly when I showered and found no soap, washcloth or towel to wipe with.

Again, I would find myself in these low places without even the basic necessities and no one to hold me and tell me it will be okay. I felt so alone and retreated to thoughts of my dad and how I was "left" without him. He should be here as an outlet for me to turn to. I had become estranged from my family and sunk further inside the hardened shell I created as my world.

Stricken with fear and filled with despair, I decided that life just wasn't worth living. I had lost all hope and just wanted all of everything to go away. Even if that meant I had to go away with it.

I remember finding a knitted belt that belonged to Denise; it was quite long. In the kitchen, there hung a ceiling fan. I took a chair from the table and dragged it beneath the fan. I climbed up on that chair and wrapped one end of the belt around the fan and the other end around my neck. I stood on that chair for the longest time.

In one sense, I wanted to do it but in another sense, I didn't want to die. I just wanted someone to notice me and care about whether I lived or died.

After probably about a half an hour, teetering around on this chair...I had been bawling and thinking of a whole host of disgusting thoughts, I began to wobble on the chair when I decided this wasn't really what I wanted. Reaching above my head to untie from the fan, the chair tipped and actually came out from under me without my consent.

For a split second, I thought, "Oh Shit!" I managed to lose my balance and the chair flipped and left me dangling and beginning to convulse, and just then, the belt I was using, broke! I remained there, curled up in a fetal position and cried and wailed of my situation. I can't even describe the feelings in my heart. I felt like I had died but here I was still breathing.

Denise never noticed that her belt was missing and I never offered up any information. She and Dave did try to help me from time to time. Dave was great friends with a guy named Andy.

During a party they had thrown after barely moving in, they introduced us. He was tall, handsome and he rode a motorcycle, which I found very masculine. He was a good guy. He had just graduated that year in June and was pursuing a career in electrical work. He was in an apprentice program about thirty minutes away and learning the trade that he would share with his father.

He came from a good family and was absolutely crazy about me. He told me that I was as cute as a bug in a rug. He wasn't crude or filthy, just a sweet, all-American boy from Auburn, Maine. We had some great times; I enjoyed riding on the back of his motorcycle when we reached speeds of 100 miles per hour around Lake Auburn.

Yes, it was dangerous, but I don't think we ever thought, "We could get killed doing this!" It was fun and everything always ended up okay. We continued to date for less than a month, but we were both pleased with our current choice.

After running around, working, partying nightly, I found a small window of time for some sleep. I was awakened by Denise. As she stood over me, her eyes were full of tears. I quickly sat up and asked her what the matter was. She said, "Heidi, Andy was killed on his way to work this morning!" He wiped out on his motorcycle and died.

I immediately began to bawl and became very angry. Here I was being hurt again. Being left behind by someone I cared a lot about. Another little piece of my heart had been chipped off.

I was in disbelief that this much bad could be happening to one person. I wondered what I did to deserve all this pain. I didn't handle it well at all; I retreated even further into my shell and didn't eat, sleep or work for days. It was like being a zombie, dead inside without thought or feeling, but still able to walk in human form.

After a few days passed, I was informed a little more about the accident. I was told that he passed a car; and upon re-entering the lane, he hit a bit of soft sand in the middle of the road that sent him sliding. As the bike went down, he stayed with it and slid under a guardrail of twisted iron rope. This caught underneath of his helmet and decapitated him leaving his helmet to be found some 20 feet from his body. He had also completely severed his arm from his body.

The detail of all of this was more than my heart could take. His father, travelling only seconds behind him, came up on the scene of the accident and recognized Andy's bike and questioned, "Where is my son?" I can't imagine what must have been going on for him internally.

My heart went out to his family. I learned that they were not telling his mother of the decapitation in an effort to protect what little bit of sanity she may have had left after learning she had lost her child. I write about him some 20 years later and the tears well up in my eyes and the pain strikes at my heart as if it just happened. I will never forget Andy and all the fun we had in such a short time. He will forever live in my heart.

The days were now passing and the despair deepened. I went on to find myself becoming more and more self-destructive. While alone in the apartment on a given night that Denise and Dave were not home, I looked to a serrated edged knife to end all of my troubles. I began to cut my wrists but not deep enough to amount to anything, just another plea for attention, I guess. I wanted to be gone but couldn't bear the thought of everyone else going on without me. A very twisted set of emotions that I didn't know how to deal with.

In a sense, this is when the "sickness" of me started. The last thing I needed or wanted was another guy trying to weasel his way into my life without an invitation. So, I'm walking up the hill to go to work and that guy, Richie from school, sees me and has his friend pull over so he can talk/hit on me. I had thought he was someone of interest before, but I wasn't into hooking up with anyone at this point.

He had an air about him that either I was going to fall head-over-heels in love with him or I would despise his very being. I was confused and still healing emotionally from Andy's death. I told Richie that I had to go to work but would be home later.

He was persistent; I'll give him that. Upon clocking out from my shift that evening, he caught up with me as I walked to my apartment. We hooked up and he asked me to go for a ride with him. He also had a motorcycle and I was very apprehensive about climbing onto the back of it. In spite of what had just happened to Andy, I did. We went for a short ride and talked very little. When it was time to bring me home, he asked me if I was hungry since he was stopping for an Italian sandwich and offered to buy me one as well. I totally played it off as if I wasn't really hungry even though my stomach was growling so loudly that I feared he would hear it.

We went back to my apartment. I didn't want him to stay; I just wanted to be alone for a while. However, I wanted the sandwich and took it with me upstairs as we parted ways in the parking lot.

After the security door downstairs closed and I was safe in my apartment, I began to woof down that sandwich like I hadn't eaten for days, which was true, I hadn't. The buzzer from the security door went off as I am plowing down my sandwich, the one I said I didn't want, and I pushed the button to unlock the door, thinking it was Denise coming home from work and misplaced her key. A knock at the door came and freaked me out because I knew it was him. I didn't want to answer the door. I had Italian sandwich breath and he would know that I lied when I said I wasn't hungry.

Truth is, I was beyond starving but I didn't want to eat in front of him. Stupid, I know, but it was a pet peeve that I had and I was not confident to partake in a messy sandwich while he watched me.

So, I had to open the door and I was so embarrassed. He was only there for a short time but I think he noticed how desperate I was but had no idea the huge bite of pride I had just swallowed. I didn't need anybody to "help" me do anything. If I didn't have something and couldn't get it on my own, I would suffer without it before taking a handout. I was not a charity case and I wasn't looking for someone to take care of me, but maybe I really was.

At this point, I just felt like he was pressing a little too hard to get with me and it was a turnoff...I was actually a little repulsed by him and I wished he would go away even if he took the sandwich with him. So, he ended up leaving and I stayed clear of him for months to come.

A few more weeks passed and winter was upon us, I had put up a valiant effort to remain on my own but I realized I was losing the battle. I couldn't go back home to my mother's house, so I called my oldest sister, Debbie, and asked her if I could come live with her for a bit. She had my nephew and was a single mom with her own apartment.

Things started looking up when I moved in with them. I was eating well and the apartment was furnished nicely with all the necessities that I had been without for so long. Things that we take for granted since they are accessible to us.

I can tell you that as a young female, I appreciated my sister furnishing me with the simplicity of sanitary napkins when it came time for my monthly period. It sure beat using a rolled up washcloth or mounds of 3 x 3 squares of scratchy commercial toilet paper from work or any local public restroom.

I know the meaning of being down and out. I have been destitute and this, unbeknownst to me at the time, was just the beginning of the decent into the bowels of hell that I would find myself sitting in. It was very dark and lonely, certainly not any place I would want to continue my existence.

Chapter 6

Drowning in a Sea of Hopeless Me

Christmas came and went and the New Year came screaming in with more trouble for me.

I had been working at the restaurant and walking in the freezing cold over the bridge from Lewiston to Auburn for months to keep my employment. I was moved up to waitressing now and was working the graveyard shift, 11pm-7am and making some pretty good tip money.

It all came to an end one night when I showed up for work and was approached about my inaccurate information I had furnished at the time of my hire. I thought, "Crap, they are onto me!" and they were. They knew I transposed the last two digits of my social security number and listed my age as 16 on my application, I was clearly only 15 when tax season rolled around and my information was entered into the system.

Busted and fired was what I was. Two steps forward and three back, the story of my life. The depression returned and so did Richie. It had been months since we had seen each other. We ended up hooking up and were officially dating for real by March. He was my boyfriend now and I was pretty head-over-heels for him. Like I said, I was either going to fall really hard for him or be totally turned off. I went for the head-over-heels and I made an emotional investment in him with everything I had in me.

We were dating for a brief time when I learned he was engaging in some harder drugs than pot, which we both smoked pretty heavily. His three sisters were four to six years older than him and he hung out with them and their rough crowd. He was very good friends with his sister's boyfriend, Roger and hung out down at his apartment a lot.

I joined him by invite and that was where I was introduced to my first line of cocaine. We took up snorting a little cocaine regularly as we could afford it. I had officially turned 16 years old in February and had a legitimate job at Shop n' Save Supermarket. I was earning pretty good money and sustaining a mere $100 a weekend cocaine habit. It soon became worse and my whole paycheck was owed to the coke dealer upon receipt of it. Soon, it became owed before it was earned and things began to spiral out of control. In this time frame, we had graduated from snorting to freebasing and we were both out of control.

Our relationship was sick from the onset. In the first year, he had been cheating on me, even with close friends of mine, and I had no idea. Our relationship was built on lies and deception and supported by a shaky foundation right from the beginning. We broke up and went out quite a bit but always ended back up with one another.

I moved out of Debbie's apartment, she was out of control with drug abuse too, and I couldn't help her...I couldn't even help myself. Richie and I lived here, there and everywhere. Wherever we partied on a given night was where we hung our hats. He lived with his friends and family members as well as I did. We eventually had our own place together. We rented an apartment on Park Street, downtown Lewiston. We were located in the heart of the rat and roach-infested neighborhood known as the tree streets. Birch, Maple, Pine, Spruce, they were referred to as the tree streets and were not a very reputable part of town. It was an ugly life for all that inhabited that area.

Wc were so heavily into the cocaine at this point, always looking for a way to purchase more. We wheeled and dealed and sold off anything we could for cash to buy drugs. We would have sold our souls if we thought we could get anything for them. Richie was selling pot and we were freebasing any profits that were made.

He was close friends with a fellow pot smoker who inherited one hundred and fifty thousand dollars upon his father's death. It was actually split between him and his sister at seventy-five grand each. Butch was only a pot smoker and hadn't become associated with cocaine until much later in the game. He eventually traded in the pot pipe for a coke pipe and then went on to become a thief, straight guy turned gay and then finally to prison.

We were friendly with both Butch and his sister, Vicky. She was right into the whole drug scene with the coke and all, and they were both very sharing by nature. Vicky was overweight and not a looker for sure but gave incessantly to Richie. I would later learn that she was giving him blowjobs and he was getting higher than a kite and sexually pleasured at the same time. I was lead to believe that they were just super good friends and that was it. It bothered me when I knew he was hanging out with her alone. She wasn't known as "Sticky Vicky" for no reason. She was doing anyone and everyone.

Richie was never too discerning in his taste for women, which doesn't say much for me, I guess. He was a chip off the old block. The first time his father and I met, he began howling at me and asked me if I would sit on his face. No discretion, no respect for women in general. Richie learned from the grand master. He became a whoremaster and had little regard for chivalry or a polite mannerism in the presence of a lady. Pigs, that's what they were...period!

In my own embarrassment, I also engaged in some rather "unethical" behaviors as well. While living in our apartment downtown, we didn't always have access to Butch and Vicky, and their money eventually ran out after just a short while.

How were we going to sustain our habit that we had become so accustomed to? He wasn't working, per say, and I wasn't making enough cash to prolong our out-of-control lifestyle. Clouded by the drugs and alcohol, I don't think either one of us was thinking with a sound mind.

Things really changed for me when the cocaine entered the equation. I had never felt so powerless and controlled in my life not only by my relationship but also by the substances I was putting into my body. Smoking pot and drinking beer was one thing...snorting cocaine was a whole new playing field.

Then, I started freebasing and I literally didn't know who I was anymore. I had turned into this monster with the most horrifying thoughts. Thoughts of how to lie, connive and deceive to get me my next fix. I owned nothing of any value and didn't value anything. Not even my own self: mind, body or spirit. I entertained thoughts of rolling some old person and robbing them to sustain my habit. Guess I wasn't that dark. I couldn't hurt others to get what I wanted. But, I could hurt myself.

After exhausting what I thought were all the tactics I could use, one had occurred to me that would compromise any self-respect I might have had, but that wasn't an issue since I had none. I still had a trick or two up my sleeve and I was willing to do whatever I had to in order to get high. I stood out there mostly in the dead of the night, and waited for him to come along. I would take my money and run. Sometimes it was only twenty-five or fifty bucks, but that was enough to get a quarter gram of cocaine and go back to Richie who sat impatiently waiting for me to return.

He knew what was going on and he turned a blind eye to it all. After all, he was getting high, why should he gripe? Every time I made bad choices for myself, I compromised another piece of my spirit, another piece of my soul. This lifestyle went on for a couple of years before I sought help.

I made countless trips on my 10-speed bicycle from Lewiston to Auburn in order to "score". Soper was a big time, downtown drug dealer who had a place in low income housing with his girlfriend and couple kids. He was dealing mass quantities of coke from that apartment every day.

There were always lights on since no one ever slept. These guys would stay up a week at a time. I remember returning there several times throughout the night to score small quantities since he did cater to the little guy like me. I would pull a trick and then look to buy.

It was about 2 am when I reached the apartment, threw my bike up against the wall and scaled the stairs with an uncontrollable urge inside. I was so anxious I could barely breathe. I approached the door and knocked sort of quietly. Someone answered through the door and asked me what I needed. I replied, a quarter. The door opened and a cop was staring me in the face. He went on to ask me what my name was and what was I doing there. He asked me why I was looking for a quarter.

I peered over his shoulder and saw more boys in blue and one had Soper faced down on the floor with his knee in his back and cuffs on his hands. I realized that a sting was in progress and I wanted out of there. I told the cop I was looking for twenty-five cents, you know, a quarter, to use the pay phone downstairs.

He looked right through me and knew I was lying but he told me to get the hell out of there and never come back. It was cool...I was okay. Soper ended up doing some time in the county but was let out shortly after, only to resume his "dealings" in another apartment in another part of town nearby.

Sometimes on down days, we would sleep the entire day away, from five or six in the morning till six or seven at night and then get up raring to party all over again. Richie and I shared that apartment on Park Street for such a brief time. It was a dump much like that of which I came from.

It wouldn't shock me when I would return at some point and turn the light on to find the floor covered with cockroaches. The light must have been their kryptonite since they played fifty scatter when it went on.

Exiting the shower and wrapped in a towel, I proceeded to walk toward the bedroom and on the way I encountered a rat in the kitchen that was the size of a house cat. We were located not far from the canal and all the apartments downtown were infested, that thing stood up on its haunches and I thought I was going to die. It saw me and began to scamper about in the kitchen.

Looking to move to higher ground, I leaped onto the first piece of furniture available. It wasn't much consolation though, he was so big, and he probably could have made the climb too. Thank God, he retreated back toward the kitchen. He finally exited through the cupboard underneath the sink where there was an enlarged hole around the pipe that lead down into the abyss. That was his inlet. Later, when we were sure he was gone; we stuffed the hole with towels and t-shirts to prevent another unwanted visit.

I hated this life, I wanted better for myself. Deep down inside, I knew this wasn't the way. Richie was so controlling and a master of lies and deception. While we were living together, he was committing one act after another, cheating on me with many of my so-called, friends. While living in that apartment, I learned of some of these adventures and I still couldn't bring myself to leave.

In fact, he was threatening to dump me one day and I wouldn't accept it. He commenced to walking out the door and down the street. I threw myself at his mercy and hung onto his leg as he dragged me down the sidewalk. I begged him not to leave me. He, with his heightened-ego self, literally kicked me to the curb.

Rejection was so hard for me. I don't think anyone handles it well at first; it hurts. I didn't have a real good hold on my emotions anyway and was a loose cannon most of the time. I made the worse scene with crying, howling, begging and pleading for this relationship not to end. I felt pity for myself as he left me there on the side of the street as he ran to get away from me.

I went to my brother's house where my junky Chevette sat since it was not registered or inspected and I did not have proof of insurance nor did I have a valid driver's license, for that matter.

No one was home so I found the keys and took the car, in anger, for a little ride. Driving up and down College Street in Lewiston, I just wanted to end it all. I couldn't take any more letdowns and disappointments.

After driving back and forth and contemplating where would be a good spot to put this heap off the road, I found a location that looked good to me. I wasn't going real fast, but sent that little blue shit box careening down the embankment, flipping over to its side. Police showed up and got me out. With all the violations I had against me, I think the cop must have had a soft spot and realized that I was pretty messed up emotionally. They loaded me into the ambulance and impounded my car.

I was already sporting a cast on my arm, not from the accident, but from punching a wall in anger. Richie and I had a very volatile relationship. At this point, he had manhandled me around quite a bit; little did I know that the worst was yet to come. I can't explain the force that had such control over me and my actions, but I felt helpless and at his mercy. What he said was like the word of God.

I returned to the apartment to find him there but not with open arms. I began to explain my love for him with such devastation that I ran my car off the road in an attempt to end it all if we couldn't be together. He had zero sympathy for me; in fact, he called me pathetic, psychotic, a maniac and wanted nothing to do with me. He left and after a bit, I went down the street to visit friends and look for someone to lick my wounds.

John Trepanier was a childhood friend of mine who lived in an apartment across the street from us. Talk about a maniac, this guy was a raving lunatic. He was a woodsman who had a strong back but a weak mind. He could sell pot and shotgun a can of beer in less than 5 seconds, but wasn't very educated. He was definitely an alcoholic and harbored his own anger management issues. However, he loved me to death and often referred to me as his "little sister."

When he got wind that Richie was hitting me, he came apart at the seams. Possessing the build of a grizzly bear and also the defensive nature and attack of one, he vowed to punch Richie out the next time he saw him. He didn't much like Richie to begin with and suggested I leave him since he knew I could do better.

When Richie and I had a chance to talk and patch things up later on...he came back to live with me at the apartment. A few weeks later, one night, in a drunken stupor, Trepanier shows up at our door at 2am in the morning. He is slamming his log-like arm on the door and calling Richie out, vowing to break his arm, as he did mine. Even though I am the one who punched the wall, Trepanier saw it as Richie's fault and he wanted him to suffer like I had.

John was a good friend to me and I always appreciated the protection he offered. Richie ended up calling the police and never honored John's request for him to come outside and dance. We ended up moving from the apartment in any event. We were like a couple of homeless people, living off whoever would let us in. We split and got back together several more times before I again, went to live with my sister, Debbie.

Living back with my sister seemed to get me on track somewhat. I began feeling like a live-in babysitter to my nephew, but I didn't mind. I was eating better and had a clean mattress to sleep on. I had started working at Knapp Shoe as an inspector. It was a remedial job to say the least. That's what you get when you don't have an education beyond eighth grade.

This was how my life was then and would go for a while to come. I sought out a higher education; I just didn't have any motivation and nothing positive in my life. Every time I turned around I was being hurt or let down by Richie. He would probably never know the depths of the wounds he inflicted on me.

Sure, I had options to go out with other guys...and I did. Every time I got something good going for me, he managed to enter back into the scene and fill my head and my heart full of empty promises that he would change for me. He was very good at persuading me to see things from his point of view.

I went out with a couple of different guys who lived out of town. Anyone who was a local and knew Richie, would say, "I'd like to take you out but your Richie's girl and I don't want no trouble." I felt stuck, owned and subject to being discarded at any given moment.

After getting back together for the thousandth time, we were sitting together on the couch at my sister's house where I was babysitting. Richie received a phone call from his family that his sister's boyfriend, Roger, who he was extremely close to, was killed while drinking, partying and playing Russian roulette. We went to be with his family as soon as my sister returned home.

After that day, things grew even worse. It was shortly after Roger's death that Richie became an even angrier, enraged person than he already was before. I remember us getting into a heated discussion that escalated to a full-fledged fight. It was like he had the devil in him and he was going to take it out on me, all the frustration and anger that he had bottled up inside.

He came after me and smacked me around the downstairs and proceeded to pull me up the stairs by my hair. Granted, I was a fighter too and I looked to get a few licks in as well. We ended up in the bedroom that I slept in which housed only a mattress on the floor. He punched me and kicked me and pummeled me around that room like I was a ragdoll.

At this point, I didn't know if I would leave that room alive. He was that out of control and angry as a bull. He eventually either fatigued or just had enough and left me there, swollen, red-faced, hair half pulled out, fat lip and that doesn't even begin to describe the scars that were not visible that lay across my heart, soul and dignity as a human being. I had been treated like an animal in the wild. He was always the conquering species and I fell prey to being his victim, time and time again. When was I going to learn? Apparently, not for some time to come.

So, the days continued to pass by and things never really seemed to get much better. Even Debbie and I were not getting along that great. She was so busy doing drugs that it felt like she was "checked out" most of the time anyway. She was there, but really had no idea what I was going through. We were each going through our own hell in our own separate lives.

One night, we got into it and she tried pushing me around a little bit and that wasn't about to fly at my age. I wasn't so little anymore. We tousled each other around a bit upstairs in her bedroom and I became enraged. I began trashing anything in my path. She just wanted me to leave and kicked me out on the spot. It was ten o'clock at night and I had nowhere to go.

She really angered me even more when she tossed my clothes, shoes and all my belongings over the railing of the third floor apartment we resided in. I could've killed her; she made me so mad! I continued to trash wall hangings, tabletop items, furniture as long as she kept throwing my whole world over the side of the porch.

Down the stairs I headed for the small courtyard below. As I gathered my things from the ground, I grew more and more angry. It pissed me off that my bras, panties, make-up and everything I owned was strewn all over the ground. It was getting late and I had no idea where I was going to sleep.

I called my girlfriend Michelle who I had just met and became friendly with through my new workplace. She was my savior that night. She embraced me with open arms and agreed to share her apartment with me.

She had a boyfriend named, Rob, but he didn't live there...I never would have guessed that through our meeting and coming to live with her, that I would meet Jeff. He was Rob's younger brother. He was so beautiful. He had jet-black hair, dark-brown, dreamy eyes, tall, slender build, and he was just so gorgeous.

Since Richie and I were broken up at the time and he was dealing with Roger's death and trying to find his way through all of that, I figured it was a good time to explore other possibilities as well. So I went out with Jeff a few times and he came to my sister's house to keep me company while I babysat my nephews.

Jeff was like my knight in shining armor. He had everything I was looking for in a boyfriend. He, first and foremost, had a job; he was employed at a naval shipyard in Bath, Maine. Bath Iron Works was a leading employer in Central Maine and they offered a good salary to those who could get in! I really liked him a lot.

One night, he had come to pick me up in his black 1967 Chevy stepside. While driving around on the tree streets, we, of course, ran into Richie. He saw me in the front seat of Jeff's truck at a stoplight. He pointed and ordered me to get out of the truck. Scared that if I didn't there would be trouble, I got out.

As I said before, every time I had hopes of hooking up with someone decent, Richie would appear on the scene and put a kibosh to that plan. He began to sweet talk me and provided me with all of the reasons why I should be with him and not Jeff. I was always taken in by his lies, deception and his ability to schmooze me. He was good at manipulating me in order to get me to do what he wanted. He was also very good at threatening me until I did what he said.

So again, I let another opportunity slip by me, along with so many others. Until I was willing to make different choices for myself, I would go on to endure more of the same. This was something I knew would not last forever. I just wasn't ready to get better. I hadn't hurt enough. As the story goes of the dog that lay on the rusty nail, the pain was not great enough to cause me to move from my discomfort. Yeah, it was excruciating, but it wasn't killing me, not yet!

Chapter 7

Recovery

After a few tokes and my courage built on that day when I had taken all that life could dish out and I felt like I couldn't take anymore, the suicidal feelings returned. I couldn't see what there was to live for. I was so sick and tired of trying to figure things out; nothing was going right for me. I couldn't see that there was any significance to my being; I had nothing to offer the world and absolutely zero purpose for being born. The world would be a better place without me and my problems, so I headed for a brisk walk towards "the Rockies."

This was a quarry where people went to party. It was widely known as the ultimate party spot. Many people partied at the bottom with huge bonfires and others stopped at inlets along the path that encircled the top. There were some locations where it was very steep and "rocky" below. Some had been known to fall off accidentally after having too much to drink.

I knew it was dangerous, but it seemed like a good place to just end it all. As I walked up Lisbon Street to gain entry from the top, I grew stronger in my conviction with my every step. What are the chances that my oldest sister, Debbie, would be driving up the hill just as I was? Course, I didn't realize then that God had placed her in my path to save me that day.

She pulled over and rolled down the window. She told me to get into the car and I refused. She told me several more times to get in. The traffic was now backing up behind her on a very busy street. She edged along the side of me in the car and demanded that I get in. Eventually, I got into the car.

I was so rushed with emotions at this point to what might have been if she hadn't come along. Again, I really didn't want to die but the thought of living was unbearable. I don't think I really wanted to end my life so much as the pain in it. I just didn't know how to change things; I didn't see how things could get better.

We drove to her apartment and went upstairs and she told me that I needed help and she was going to get some for me. She got in touch with Jackson Brook Institute in South Portland, Maine and they agreed to take me if I would go voluntarily.

After bantering back and forth for a while, I finally agreed to go to the facility. She wasn't kidding around; we were in the car and on our way to South Portland that evening. When I arrived and began the admissions process, Debbie hung around for a little bit but then left. I felt so betrayed, so alone. How could she do this to me? I had been dumped off at this facility and didn't even know anyone and was so scared of what was coming.

I was initially placed on the special care ward for them to evaluate my head. They had no idea of the jungle of wretched thoughts that inhabited my mind. It was quickly realized that I had instability to think, emote or feel with a cognitive mind. Before they were willing to correct my drug problem, they thought they needed to address my head problems first.

After spending some time on the psychiatric ward, I was moved to the drug unit to begin my rehabilitation. My sister had committed me; but since I was 18 years old, I could leave at my own will, but where was I going to go? So, now the fun was about to begin. They thought they were going to be able to decipher, dissect and break me down to get to the root of my problems...good luck, I thought. I shut down and would not comply with any of their requests or protocols. I became as defiant as I have ever been known to be, which I had a very colorful past at this point, mind you.

Every time I met with any psych techs (PTs), they would try to pick my brain and ask me questions to gain clarity of who I was and what plan of action it was going to take to get me functioning again. I thought it was a big waste of time and wouldn't cooperate with their unending questions. Every inquiry entailed, "How does that make you feel?" I was extremely irritated by them asking me that same question over and over again. What did they know about my altered state of mind? All they knew was what they had read from some textbook. I was infuriated when they would offer up detailed reasons for my behavior. I thought, "Oh please! You have no idea what it is like to have your mind, body, thoughts, feelings, basically your entire life taken over by drugs and alcohol." I would reply, "Don't try to tell me that you understand where I am at, because you have no f*cking clue."

This went on for the first couple of weeks until I met Rocco. He was a group leader in a controlled forum that encouraged you to talk about your feelings. He provoked thought and really got your wheels turning in a healthier direction. Rocco was a recovering addict by his own admission. He had a genuine sense about him that you just knew he has been where you are right now. He turned it around and so could I. He was a no bullshit kind of guy. He didn't want to hear excuses that your deal was harder than someone else's. He taught us to pull ourselves up by our own bootstraps and get with the program. I liked him and I identified with him and therefore, I listened to him.

From that first session forward, I began to make strides in my recovery. I was attending, AA, NA,

CA (alcoholics, narcotics and cocaine anonymous) along with every other "a"-ending meeting you can think of, but something changed. I wasn't just present as a warm body in the room; I was really listening.

I learned the 12-step philosophy to recovery and began to "buy in" to this theory. Opening up and sharing became easier for me. Rocco had inspired me, which few people, if anyone, had ever done for me up until that point. I felt a connection to him from one addict to another. He could talk the talk but he walked the walk as well.

When I first came to Jackson Brook, the meetings were chaired by a chosen individual, who showed signs of leadership through their sobriety process.

In the beginning, I looked at the current, "Mayor" of JBI and thought, "Wow, that person has really made strides to be holding that position." In the weeks to come, I would earn the role as Mayor of JBI, a role I never thought possible for me.

Just like everyone before me, I eventually finished my program and had to face the inevitable task of reentering society. It was scary to think about being out there "in population" where I could make choices for myself and no longer had the sheltered environment that had blanketed me for the last thirty-something days.

Regardless of my readiness, I left the institution and returned back to the familiar. Premeditated usage of drugs was referred to as a "slip." I learned all about my vulnerability and the constant fear of a slip or regression back to who I was before seeking help. One is too many and a thousand is never enough, I heard. They were right, once you took the first drink or drug it put you right back to square one to begin all over again.

Yeah, I "slipped" a few times when I got out...but I was clearly a different person with a few tools in my tool belt and I knew enough to pull them out when I needed them. As Dr. Phil says, "Some people get it and some people just don't get it." Well, I got it! It wasn't right away though. It took time.

I left JBI in August of 1987 and hooked up with my friend Angel and I decided to go to Job Corps. It wasn't returning to high school as my mother had wished; however, it was a means to educate myself and acquire my GED while learning a trade.

Some viewed it as a school for losers, people who couldn't cut it anywhere else. I might have been one step above being a loser and at the same time it seemed like a good fit for me.

I had been encouraged upon leaving rehab not to revisit my old playgrounds...steer clear of old party buddies, etc. Those people and places were toxic for me and detrimental to my recovery.

This list included my very co-dependent relationship with Richie. He was out of rehab now too. In fact, he stayed in our hometown of Lewiston for his care and barely stayed a week or better. I was really just looking to make a clean break from everyone and everything, including him.

Job Corps was located 3 hours north of Lewiston in the town of Bangor. I never thought Richie would follow me there, but input day rolled around every Tuesday and about a month into it, guess who came walking through the door, yup, Richie. I don't know what the hold was he had over me but I had made attempts to "get away" just to find myself cornered by him again.

My grandmother would always say, "You know...but you don't do as well as you know!" She spoke these words, which was a fair description of my behavior. Somewhere deep down inside, I knew that he wasn't good for me. I didn't have the strength to go with what I knew was in my best interest.

With the exception of people who suffer with mental and cognitive impairment and those under the influence of mind-altering substances and without all faculties, we all have that inner voice, conscience, sixth sense or whatever anyone wants to call it that moves us in one direction or another. For me, when I was stone sober, I did have the ability to think rational and discern between right and wrong and I would continue to make bad choices time and time again. They were my choices to make and I learned not to blame anybody else for where my life was and where it is now.

So, after I earned my GED at Job Corps, I decided to break free from Richie again and go back to Lewiston. Of course, he followed me...again. I was still experiencing some "slips" after coming out of rehab, not while I was in Job Corps, well, maybe a little pot here and there but certainly no cocaine. When I returned to Lewiston, it was like the familiar sucked me in and I used a few more times before the end was in sight.

Chapter 8

Marrying the Monster

In the spring of 1989, I became pregnant with my first son, Travis. I really didn't have any money or a stable relationship and was still hanging out with my pot-smoking friends. One of which I took an apartment with on Bartlett Street in downtown Lewiston. His name was Mike and we were just friends. He had a very caring sense about him and helped me through some rough times. Neither one of us had two nickels to rub together.

He had a clunker for a car that was up on blocks more than it was mobile. I quit the shoe shop and took a job at Country Kitchen bakery. It was a huge plant that manufactured bread, rolls and baked goods. Problem was, as I got further along in my pregnancy, the heat would be so intense that I just couldn't work there anymore. I lived in that apartment for the duration of my pregnancy.

Times were so tough; I didn't have a job and therefore, no money. My parents came down to see me and often took me back to their house where I would stay for weeks at a time. My mom had remarried a man from Jay, Maine, who became my stepdad. His name was Buddy; and for 20 years, he would be the closest thing to a real dad that I would ever know. He truly is the best father that I could have ever asked for.

They helped me a lot and I appreciate everything they did for me. Meanwhile, on my return trips back to Lewiston, I was yearning to be with Richie. After all, he was the father of my unborn child, even though he was denying it every step of the way. He really shut me out for most of my pregnancy. He would come sniffing around when he wanted to get laid and then he would disappear for weeks at a time. He accused me of sleeping around and was certain that this baby wasn't his.

Remember, I had been seeing Jeff prior to this time and Richie was sure that he was the father of my child. He just never really wanted to accept responsibility for his part in all of this. He remained estranged until Travis was born.

On January 16, 1990, Richie reentered my life with full force and walked around proud as a peacock the day Travis was born. He wasn't there through all the hardships but was sure to cash in on the glory.

I remained in the apartment for six months after the birth of Travis. I had gained a sense of esteem and confidence that I could do this alone and I didn't need Richie's help. After all, he hadn't even been around for the last nine months anyway.

I was in close contact with my folks and they became even more involved once the baby arrived. They came and picked me up and brought me to their house, where I spent much of my time as a new mother. I began trying to rebuild my life and applied for low-income housing for me and Travis, conveniently located only two miles from my parents.

Something happened to me as a person after I had the baby. It was as if God had put the "party brakes" on and said, "Time to get off and start being responsible." I had another life to care for other than my own. Someone else who needed me and depended on me and I couldn't let him down. I thought, "I finally have someone who I can call my own and no one can take him away from me." He will love me no matter what and he will never leave me like the others have in the past. I fell in love with Travis; and for the first time in my life, I loved something more than I had ever experienced before.

By June, we had moved to Wilton, Maine into that subsidized apartment complex near my folks. It was a nice place to make our new start, which is what I had intended for Travis and I.

I had remained in contact with my childhood best friend, Tina. I asked her not to tell Richie where I was since I was really attempting to get on with my life, without him. That worked for about a month and she eventually told him where I was. He quickly came calling on me and again, reentered my life through the revolving door to my heart.

I tried to be strong but somehow he always managed to persuade me. It always seemed, that when things grew tough, he would make his exit; and when he learned of anything good that I had going on, he would materialize again. I think I was convenient for him and he could get some needs met from me from time to time, otherwise he had another agenda, another "secret" life.

Oh, and a secret life he did live. I would go on to find out more than I wanted to. He took a job at the tannery in Wilton, one of the few places to work in such a small town. He continued to sell dope as he did in high school and throughout our relationship. The partying never stopped and my apartment began to feel like a flophouse for him and his low-class friends.

We fought all the time and constantly pulled in opposite directions. We carried on this way; and in the fall, I became pregnant with our second son, Luke. Both of my pregnancies were not very eventful. I was going through changes physically, mentally and really never enjoyed being "barefoot and pregnant."

While carrying Travis, Richie was not present much so I had a different set of feelings than when I had Luke. I knew he was with other women the first time around. All my friends were keeping me informed of his whereabouts and shenanigans.

However, when I was carrying Luke, we had made a pact to start anew and do things right. What a joke! For me, it was watching him have a continuation of the party in progress. While I was growing up and realizing that my behavior had to change, he kept on with the same old, same old. I will never forget the heart-wrenching day that I received a phone call from a woman explaining in detail of her affair with Richie.

How could he do this to me? I was pregnant with his child, we were together; we had a decent place to live, finally. I sat on the stairs, big belly and all and cried, no wailed, with a cry I had never heard before. I was experiencing something I had not felt before, a series of events were changing me and I had work to do.

This may have been a turning point for me that would alter my course forever. I could feel my spirit breaking and I was losing touch with my very being. This had to stop, but how? Birth and death are a bit synonymous in my situation, a part was dying inside but a new me was about to be born.

I don't know how I managed through those late night calls and he was panting as if he was engaging sexually at the moment and wanted me to hear it. Those kinds of scars never go away. I would rather take a punch to the face, which I did, than to have my emotional state of mind abused to that degree.

I certainly did put up with a lot. He had convinced me over years of verbal abuse that I was a dumb, no good, a slut, whore and bitch who was not deserving of anything. I already had very low self-esteem. Having been raised in a similar environment, I didn't need any convincing.

Ok, so here I am twenty-one years old with two children by a man who didn't want to marry me and had very different goals and aspirations in life than me. A couple more years would pass and I worked on him to get married and become a real family.

In 1993, we married and I knew it was a mistake. Did you ever do something and while you are in the midst of it, you get a strong intuitive feeling that this is wrong and you should not move forward? This was my wedding day.

With every step I took toward him, God was telling me that this is a mistake, don't do it, turn back now! I didn't listen to my internal voices, instead, I thought, shut up...and I continued to march on. All the indicators were there and I chose not to listen. Why are some women, including myself, convinced we can change, shape and mold our "bad boy" into the perfect prince?

Right off the bat, when you look at someone as a potential mate, it is a good idea to start by not compromising your standards and believing that you can "fix" the things about that person that you don't like. Wow, I had a lot to learn about relationships.

Two years flew by so fast. I was now twenty-three years old and still had no idea of what a good working relationship was comprised of. Like most information I have come by, it has been through reading materials. I once met an influential gentleman in my life who told me, "Knowledge is power! So, get to the library and get reading."

For a couple more years, I would stagger around in darkness trying to find my own way. One very strong impulse had visited me several times before now and that was the yearning to have a relationship with God.

I was raised to never fall powerless to anything or anyone. To accept that there could be something or someone that had higher powers over me was a concept that I wasn't too sure I wanted to become submissive to. I guess this is why whenever I got that intuitive nudge, I would resist. Well, it became so strong that I couldn't ignore it anymore.

The author that presented himself to me first was Robert Schuller. It was as if the book jumped off the shelf at the library and into my hands. It was entitled, *You Are Loved*. I had no idea how much the Lord loved me and I felt like I had come home into His arms where I would be safe for eternity.

This was really the turning point for me and my life. The more I read, the more empowered I felt. I began to feel a sense of worth and purpose. I understood that God made me in His image and that made me worthy regardless of anything else. Coming from a lifetime of low self-esteem and low self-worth, I had a hard time to accept that my worthiness was granted to me as my birthright. I thought you had to perform perfectly in order to be worthy. I had behaved rather badly up to this point and sentenced myself to more despair in an effort to pay for my sinful behavior. God was willing to accept me just the way I was and loved me unconditionally.

I began reading more authors such as Brian Tracy, Norman Vincent Peale, Gary Null, Marianne Williamson and many others. Through them, I became inspired and began to recognize that there really was light at the end of the tunnel. I had been raised up with only a smidgen of exposure to religion on my father's side of the family. What they stood for didn't resonate with me and that was definitely not my way home.

I began attending a Baptist church in the town I lived in. Richie didn't like any of this growth that I was experiencing. I think it posed a threat to him to no longer impact me with his negative influence. I was gaining strengths I had never had before. He didn't want me going to this church, but my faith was stronger than his will. He denied me from taking our two sons, but I eventually did take them and we were unified by the power of God's love. It often felt like me and the boys were a separate entity from him. Travis, Luke and I would go on to be baptized and accept Jesus into our hearts.

Nothing has been the same since. Through Him, I can do anything. He is the one constant that is there for me no matter if I am showing my good or bad self. I am so thankful for all the wonderful works He has performed in my life. Early in my spiritual journey, I would find myself asking God for signs to reassure that I am on the right track. I don't really know where I learned to do this, but I do it all the time. I ask Him to communicate through signs, feelings, thoughts, intuitive voice or any connective way to let me know if I am thinking the right way. I originally asked for a deeper belief of His existence and this is what happened. I asked whether He was real or not and to show me something that would impact me enough to believe.

I was driving up a street; and as I approached a slight incline, a tractor-trailer truck emerged from the peak of the hill with only its fairing showing and as big as life it read, "G.O.D." in large black letters. That was all the convincing I needed.

It turned out to be a guaranteed overnight delivery truck and it certainly delivered in a big way that day. Since that day, my faith has wavered from time to time and I would fall away from The Lord several more times throughout my journey. Jesus always remains steadfast in my life. My Heavenly Father is the one constant that never lets me down and never gives up on me. I still ask for signs and guidance for everything in my life.

As I began to trust in the Lord, I, in turn, began to trust in myself as well. I started to see that I could rely on Jesus to guide me and I had the ability to choose to exercise my own judgment instead of waiting for someone else to make decisions for me.

By the time I reached adulthood and had started a family of my own, the partiality toward me was spiraling out of control but I did not realize it since I was in the center of the stage. Emotions and circumstances concerning my feelings were clouding my ability to see what was really going on. Sometimes it takes for us to detach ourselves from the situation in order to view it more clearly.

As I mentioned earlier, upon the birth of my first son at nineteen years old, I moved into subsidized housing about two and a half miles away from my mother and stepfather. My mother was thrilled to say the least. The more involved she could secrete herself into my life, the better for her.

At this point in my adult life, this only summoned for yet another vicious game of favoritism, with me placed at center stage, again. My mother spent a lot of time at my house during those years. Since I was not married and struggling as a single mom, she helped me immensely.

As a teenager, just a couple of years prior to this period, I had not struck up a lot of votes in my favor that I would ever amount to anything in life. I had become enthralled in a life of drugs, alcohol and a not so glorious lifestyle. I was a loser; everyone knew it, including me.

I became pregnant and that changed everything. From that point forward, I made many strides to turning my life around and making something out of the mess I had created. Notice, I said, "I." I do not blame anyone, including my mother, for my choices.

Parents are role models, the most impactful influence over their children. I was dealt a negative hand and I played accordingly. The day I gave birth to my baby boy, I realized that I was now that influential person and I wanted to show him better than what I was shown. I had the ability to change the rules according to how I thought they should be. I was becoming empowered and aware of defective behaviors, both mine and others who surrounded me.

My family did not have a lot of faith in me; but as I began to display a 360-degree turn around with my life, I had truly "Wow' d" many of them and gained respect through my actions.

I was doing much better now and Richie had reentered my life in hopes to come play house with our brand new son. He never was very serious about parenthood or creating a family environment. Travis would bear my last name until the age of three before Richie was ordered to take a paternity test that would prove his role in his child's life. In fact, our second son had been born by this time and was a year and a half waiting for his father to step up and claim him as well.

All the while, my mother was privy to most everything that was going on in my life. She babysat the children so that we could work and I paid her off in trade by cleaning her house and helping with chores she needed done.

The relationship was at an unhealthy status and I couldn't see it. Every bit of time she spent with me and my family was being relayed to my other four siblings through phone conversations and visits to their homes.

She would go to their homes and talk incessantly about Heidi, Richie and the boys. She would tell them how smart Travis and Luke were and enlighten them of everything they did, said or were involved in — to the point where she ignored their children and anything that was going on in their lives.

She especially talked me up and boasted about what a wonderful mother, housekeeper, worker, wife, daughter and person I was. She placed me up on a pedestal to the others and put me so out of touch with all of them.

On countless occasions, they informed her of their feelings concerning her partiality. She would deny it and defend her position by saying she boasts about all her children and grandchildren. She downplayed the legitimacy of their complaints, which made them feel ignored even more.

While continuing to brag my kids and me up, she induced hatred toward me by my siblings. I wish I could attribute her behavior to ignorance but it is more about the way she was raised and learned behavior. She never subscribed to the fact that she could break the cycle if she would just take ownership of the fact that it is what it is, now do something about it! That is the road less traveled; it is easier to just go the same way as others have before you.

Her father's side of the family were ones to show favoritism. They did it in a very open and hurtful fashion. If they could think of something nasty to say that would make you feel lesser than someone else, they would *knowingly* say it! It was shear evil and uncalled for and has hurt so many people even after most of them have perished. Shame on those who continue to carry that torch and choose not to put an end to this unacceptable behavior.

My maternal grandmother was at the mercy of this cruelty for many years. My grandfather was unkind with his words, was nasty and downright malicious with his mouth. He was mean to her in that sense, always cutting her to the quick. A most fantastic woman that did not come from that background, whatsoever! He was very fortunate to be graced with her presence all the days of his life. Like her mother, my Nanny, she would never have a callous word to say about anyone. She was an offspring of two of the most kind, gentle and wonderful people who ever inhabited God's green earth.

It is too bad that my mother and her four sisters all turned out to be replicas of their father. They are all cynical, critical and often times, very cutting with their mouths.

Ladies, it is time to take ownership if you want to change these circumstances. Dr. Phil says, "You can't change what you don't acknowledge." This is your wake-up call! My mother has always been judgmental, overbearing to say the least and Relentless with a capital "R!" Growing up in this environment has instilled many of her undesirable traits into my character. I always say, "Children learn what they live!" I have had to battle with my own inner demons to change the things I don't like about me. It has required a lot of self-examination and dissection of my behaviors and where they derived from. You CAN change if you so desire to, but it will not come without a price, it all comes down to sheer will and effort.

We only lived a couple of miles from my mother and my stepdad; and through my own fault, I had allowed my mother to become way too involved in my married life. She knew everything there was to know and I had furnished her with all the information. She spent a lot of time at my house, as I said earlier; she helped out watching the two boys as Richie and I worked opposite shifts. If she wasn't at my house, then I was at hers. I cleaned my own house and also hers. It felt like an even trade off, she babysat and I maintained her housekeeping.

I was always looking for her approval and to gain a little praise if I could. Why could she tell everyone how great I was, everyone except me? All of my life, it always seemed that no matter what I offered her for achievement, she found fault with it. I could have done it better if it was this way or that way; there was always some sort of criticism that accompanied her opinion of my performance.

It wasn't only her, who followed over the top of my head, like a dark rain cloud, it was Richie, too! I came to identify that these two people had absolutely no goals of their own and therefore it was detrimental for me to share mine with them. Anything that I had aspiration to do was shot down by their pessimistic attitudes and lack of personal incentive.

It is hard to move forward and upward when you have negative forces working against you. Hard, I said, but not impossible! Many people use this as an excuse not to get off their duff and make things happen for themselves. My advice, listen to your own intuitive self; it knows you best and what's best for you. It always has your best interest at heart and is fully invested in you and your success in everything you do. Don't wait for others to give you the okay to do something, step out, step up and make it happen!

I had a lot of negative forces in my life that mounted the reasons, higher than I could stand, why I couldn't or shouldn't do this or that. People set limits on themselves and then they try to impress their disbelief on you. Today, I am the one who sets my own limits. I raise the bar high and always look to Be, Have or Do...MORE! Some people in my life were just plain toxic for me. As you succeed and others witness your ability, some will become jealous and they become the naysayers. Avoid these people, regardless of their position in your life. It is hard, but you will be a healthier, happier person as a result. People are, who and what they are, regardless of their role in your life.

You must be willing to pull the trigger if you don't want to be weighted down by others' gloom and doom tactics. All of this growth has taken place in my life since I was urged by a friend to begin reading. He came into my life for a reason...he encouraged me to invest in a tool that I would use many times throughout my life. If you are currently struggling with an unwanted situation and wish for it to get better, I recommend that you visit your local library and start gaining power through reading.

Chapter 9

The Healing Begins

I was working for Bass Shoe at the time, which employed many people in the Wilton area. There wasn't a whole lot of commerce to sustain the population; a local tannery was about the only other business besides shoe manufacturing that kept this dry town alive. The shoe shop was a very unfulfilling job. It was very mundane in its nature and the environment was one of a rough culture. The overall general morale was low amongst workers. Fights were subject to break out at any point and people bickered and squabbled daily. Foul language, dirty talk, inappropriate behaviors and gestures took place as common practice, becoming known as "Shop Talk." It was never an encouraging atmosphere and didn't foster a very professional culture.

Throughout my short career of about a year and a half, we were notified that Bass would be closing the doors soon. Or at least it began as rumor for sometime before the doors actually closed. Over a period of time, I began to notice that the orders were not as big and sections of the warehouse were empty and lines were closing down. I began to get concerned that I would be losing my job and felt I should take a proactive approach to set myself up with something else to avoid an unemployment period. I could not afford to be out of work, we needed every penny that was earned in order to just keep our heads above water, no extras.

It was a blessing when word came that Walmart was moving to the neighboring town of Farmington. I saw this as an opportunity to go from the shop to the store without missing a beat in between. So, instead of waiting for Bass to put me in the unemployment office, I resigned after landing a position with Walmart.

I was hired as a seasonal employee through the holidays and then became a full-timer after Christmas. I was working soft lines, which was the clothing department. I was offered a position on the receiving team which meant I would work from 9:00pm-7:00am. It was hard, laborious work to palletize freight out of an 18-wheeler, especially when things were just thrown in there and had to be sorted out.

Something was just always not right with being awake when the rest of the world was sleeping. I did this for about a year, ran off very little sleep so I didn't miss the things that Travis and Luke were doing. I had also taken a night job at the local convenience store to earn a bit more money.

We simply just didn't have enough to make the weekly bills. Life was so scary then, we would have to choose between paying the bills in full and buying the essentials like bread and milk. Somehow, I knew we would not go under, because I would work my fingers to the bone to prevent that. However, it was painful to want more for the kids and all of us and have to go without.

I always managed to keep the boys from knowing that we were poor. They may not have had all brand name clothing, some were Faded Glory from Walmart and others from Ames, coordinated with a pair of Nikes, and they never realized that they didn't have much.

My life had been a huge sacrifice from the beginning of time so I didn't miss what I never had. Those boys were my life and everything that moved me was through them. I thank them for being great kids and motivating me to keep on pressing forward when I had nothing left in me.

Sometimes you can be right on the cusp of success and you give up, whereas, had you known how close you were, you might have been able to find a little more in you, somewhere deep within. This was my motto...my feeling and my mindset. I know I'm close and therefore I will continue to press forward. This led me to believing that I could do more; I could do better than what I was currently doing.

The twin cities of Lewiston/Auburn had a little more to offer than the town of Wilton where I resided. I decided to apply for a job where I thought the pay might be a little better. Richie had taken a job at a company called Americon. They built truck caps, stairs, bed liners and boats out of fiberglass. It was a dirty job, as I am sure, Mike Rowe would agree. In very hot temperatures, a suit of paper would be worn over the top of your clothes, along with gloves, boots, respirator and head/eye protection.

I still can't figure out for the life of me, why this job was at all desirable to me. I applied anyway and was hired to gel coat repair boats, say what...How do you do that? I had no experience but they were willing to train me and they portrayed a sense of relief that they could teach me "their" way of doing things and I had no bad habits of the trade to overcome.

After several months, I found myself hating this job and looking for a way to improve my situation. While on my 15-minute break, I lay back in a pile of rubble and gazed around at the filthy environment I had put myself in. It was at this moment that I heard an advertisement for Central Maine Technical College on the radio. I had probably heard it before, but it really struck a chord with me right then and there.

Sometimes we can have information present itself many times and in many ways and it is at that opportune time that the stars align or something happens that we hear what's being played over and over. My receptors were wide open and allowing this energy to flow into my consciousness.

Of course, when the idea had occurred to me prior to this day, I had been told by "others," namely, Richie, that I couldn't go to college. That hurt since this was always a dream of mine. I missed my opportunity at traditional age, my own stupidity, especially since I was a recipient of Social Security benefits due to the death of my father. I had college tuition paid for me, no worries.

Whatever the circumstances, as I matured and became more willing to take responsibility for my life, I really yearned for a higher education. It was crushing when Richie tried to go to college before me. I think he only went because he knew how bad I wanted to go. Always trying to one-up me, his endeavor ended about as quickly as it started with complete and utter failure.

A classic example of when your heart isn't really invested and you lack passion; failure lurks in the shadows waiting to present itself. You get out what you put in; you reap what you sow, whatever the cliché. God knows of your intentions and will proceed accordingly, every time!

So, I answered the ad I heard on the radio. I went to the admissions office and spoke with a gentleman about my quest. We talked for a bit and he laid it out to me what it would take to walk out of there with a two-year degree. Mind you, I worked 40+ hours a week and had two boys who were 7 and 8 years old. Therefore, I could not do a regular schedule of course studies.

He explained to me that this two-year degree would not be attainable for about 3.5 years if I were to take three classes per semester. I knew it wasn't going to be easy, I would continue to work and go to school 3 to 4 nights a week from 6-9pm. However, before I could begin they had to know how much I knew. I would have to return for testing in the fields of mathematics and reading comprehension.

The day came and I returned to test my current knowledge. I aced the reading comprehension but failed miserably on the math. I needed to place in the 35 percentile in order to pass the entrance exam and I fell short with a mere 11%.

I was so embarrassed, but I didn't quit. It was early August when I began this journey and I had to be ready to start in roughly 20 days. I went to the library and began to self teach mathematics beginning as far back as the Dewey Decimal System. I was determined to educate myself and go back until I could pass that test.

Now, I dropped out of high school remember, and so everything I was recalling was dug out of my 7th and 8th grade archives. The problems looked familiar, but if you miss one step, you are dead in the water. Upon reentering to take the exam for the second time, days before school would start; I passed the test and was ready to begin college.

I felt so accomplished and I knew that this was only the beginning of an upcoming star performance I would put on over the next few years. When you start out small with tiny goals, they begin to stack up into great successes. This is how I have lived my life, in small increments at a time, one frame at a time until the picture is complete.

I had been out of school for quite a while and I knew that this new endeavor wasn't going to be an easy one...and it wasn't! Everything was a struggle, especially since I didn't have a lot of support, none in fact. I think that fueled me even more, the reality that others didn't believe in me and actually laid out the welcome mat and awaited my demise. I thought, "I'll show them what I am capable of." When it came right down to it, the only person I was really looking to impress was me. I began to learn that everything started with me and what "I" thought about the situation, not what others said or thought. I applied this type of thinking to many areas of my life.

Through my spiritual journey, I learned that God loved me just for being me. It was my birthright to know that I am worthy. At the time, I was still smoking marijuana and I began to investigate the reasons why I was doing that. I came to realize that I was afraid to stop indulging because of what my friends might think of me. I began to dissect this issue and concluded that my opinion was the only one that really counted.

I quit smoking pot in the summer of 1997 and found that I had disciplines that I didn't even know existed. I mean, I guess I always knew I had structure, regiment and a routine to my life once I became a parent. It had been there all the while and I just never paid any attention to it. Keeping my kids and my home and being disciplined in those areas just seemed to come natural to me.

They are all the ways I still am today. Things that are hard to quit or get started required strengths that had been buried in a low self-esteem. The best part is that once you start putting some order to some of the havoc in your life, you pick up small bits of momentum and each task becomes less difficult. Whenever I am about to make a decision on anything, I immediately place myself at the front lines and ask, "How is this going to affect me?"

When you are able to learn to love yourself and be your own best caretaker, your world can become one of comfort and ease. It's all about doing things that make you feel great and also walk in line with your core values. When you get a warm, fuzzy feeling and the lights are all green, you should move forward. It's when the lights are red, things are very difficult, you feel uneasy about the situation and your inner voice, your conscience, will not stop plaguing you. Harmony is relatively easy and it doesn't feel like work.

Things always have a way of working out. I had been walking around in darkness for many years, not believing in myself and my ability. I have recently come to grips with the fact that I have been hiding for most of my life. Yeah, things are difficult especially when the reward is handsome. I had been hiding from any true purpose in life, claiming that my potential was in being Travis and Luke's mother. As long as I convinced myself that God put me on this earth only to be a mother and nothing else, well, I stunted any possibilities of contributing my many talents to the world. I do realize that I am here for a greater good, since the children eventually leave the nest and then what is anyone to do? Fear can absolutely paralyze you and hold you back from being all that you can be.

As I look back, I see that not some, but all, the successes came as a result of a failure. Also, it is almost certain that great success will come from many small achievements. For example: I quit drugs and alcohol and laid down the cigarettes, attended college for a higher education, did a 180-degree turn with my life, and well, you get the idea. These accomplishments happened over a span of ten years and were not achieved simultaneously.

Sometimes, when you have a long laundry list of things to work on, it can become overwhelming to the point of paralysis. If you start small and see just one thing through to completion, you will gain strength to take on the next and the next. Failure must be present if success is to be had. Nothing will come without working for it. It is mainly my positive outlook that has summoned all of the goodness in my life. However, you can't have one without the other. A positive attitude with no effort will not get you what you are looking for. Which brings me back to the negative relationships that were present in my life...all the positive thinking in the world was not going to fix these issues until I decided to take action, (work) to weed them from my life.

So, at this point, I had landed a decent job for a printing company. I had been working there for about a year and a half. It was, by far, the best job I had ever held and I enjoyed what I was doing. Having a feeling that there was more out there for me, I was invited to attend a career briefing with an insurance company. I visited this new opportunity and saw the potential for me to work more independently and have more control over my income based on my efforts.

A wise person once told me, "No Risk...No Reward!" I understood that if I wanted to move ahead, I had to be willing to let go. After conducting my due diligence on this new endeavor, I decided to quit my job and take the offer. I asked God that night before resigning if this is what he wanted for me. The answers I got were all directed toward moving forward. I had no idea how things would turn out but I resolved that I would work my hardest, as always, and trust in my faith that God would not steer me wrong, and he never has.

So, now it appears that I have this great opportunity in front of me, however, I truly wasn't prepared at this point in my life to make this acceptance. Besides, being tentative to letting go of the good thing I already possessed, I did not have a rainy day fund that would help sustain me while building my book/client base in a commissions-based employment. I just really did not have a very good support system in place, and one is as essential as the other. Timing is everything and I felt like my clock was broken.

Chapter 10

Lessons Learned

Keep in mind that, as you make your ascension up the ladder of success, many relationships may not be able to withstand your accomplishments.

One of the most troubling parts of this is that many of the hands that I have extended in the past have come back to slap me in the face. Ouch! I tried to help everyone I could even when I didn't have that much myself. Sometimes it would come in the way of time since that was what I had more of than money or any other commodity. I gave willingly of my time and sacrificed much along the way. But, through all of this, the jealousy monster had reared its ugly head several times. The envy that some of my closest friends and family members possess has been greater than the love for our relationship. It is the root of all evil second to pride. I understand this and have learned to proceed accordingly concerning those people.

The underlying point is to concentrate on making yourself happy first and then you will be great for others. I was always trying to be the people pleaser and that almost never worked since no one can be pleased all of the time and some people can't be pleased any of the time. Taking care of my needs, in a healthy manner, is required and is not to be confused with selfishness. You have the right to love yourself and not always come second to others and their desires.

So, is there a message in all of this? The answer is yes; there is a method to my madness. I didn't fill these pages with the stories of my life and the hardships I endured with any intention of gaining pity, sympathy or any kind of pardon since I had a less than magical childhood. Contrary to that, I have shared my experiences with the hope that I may inspire even one person to realize their potential as a human being and a very loved child of God. No, my row was not easy to hoe but there is always someone out there that has had it worse than you, trust me. I did not come from a fairytale upbringing; it was tough, it was hurtful and I own every bit of it because it was my life and nobody else experienced it in color through my eyes.

Everyone has a different threshold of pain and ways of dealing with things. Despair is despair, and it doesn't know tough or weak. I wish that things hadn't been the way they were but I understand that all of the circumstances and events in my life have happened for a reason. I have endured the life experiences that I have because they have shaped me and molded me into the person I am today. Without those trials and tribulations, I would not be the strong individual that I have evolved into.

Every time I stumbled and fell down, it taught me to pick myself up. Every time I failed, it was just leading me to the ways of success. I was narrowing the ways that didn't work until I found the one that did. Every time I couldn't seem to catch a break from life, I was learning how to never give up. I have learned that all of my life lessons were gifts from God; I just didn't always know it.

I am a little stubborn and a little thickheaded at times. I know that this probably comes as a surprise to you, right? Problem is, my life was like a mirror, which had fallen to the ground and shattered into a million little pieces and I hit the ground, retrieving every fragment trying to put it back together and recreate the same image as before. I believe that God gives us tests throughout our lives. He speaks to us. He gives us the opportunity to discern; and when we go against His will, things shatter and we do not learn our lesson. When this occurs, a great opportunity is presented to us and we must use it to examine why things have fallen apart, rather than concentrating on the disorder that has been created. Find in it the reason or the message you are to take from it; it is necessary or it wouldn't have happened.

Traditionally, we are taught the lesson first and then tested of our knowledge. In the game of life, we are given the test first and the life lesson comes after. Funny thing is, when you don't learn the lesson, the test is repeated to you, sometimes over and over, until you pass.

It's ok to understand that our mirrors will break and shatter all over the ground but we must learn to only pick up the pieces that create harmony and leave the ones that are no longer of use to us. We are ever-changing individuals; our mirror images transform with every passing day. Our experiences and challenges provide us with a "new look." One that reflects our current knowledge and wisdom along with our present day understanding of this game we call life and how it is played.

The prospect always exists for us to Be, Have or Do whatever we decide upon; we just need to be aware of our circumstances and know that we have the ability to become whatever we put our minds to. I look at my past and see a very different person than who I have evolved into today. My looks, my body, my thoughts, my mind and my abilities are all morphed into giving me a whole new representation of myself. The mirror image is never the same twice.

Breathe in the moments of yesterday, today and tomorrow as they will be every bit as individual as you are. Did you ever try to recreate a moment and find that you can get it pretty close, but it will never be the exact same? Like the snowflakes that fall in the wintertime, the days of our lives and our representation of "self" is never to be duplicated precisely as it was before - or ever will be again.

Embrace everyday with the intention to reveal your best version of you. My life has changed because I have become willing to listen to my inner voice of God, who is the Creator of my joy.

When I am receiving that internal nudge, I have learned to pay attention instead of dismissing it. Letting go and letting God has released me from the chains that have imprisoned me with fear. That one emotion, fear, has served as an impediment in reaching my goals. Jesus tells us that we shall not fear, be not afraid, He is with us, always! I can do nothing without The Lord, but with Him...all things are possible! Become mindful of the thoughts that you allow to fill your head. Only rent space in there for the positive and you will see great changes come about. Have a forgiving heart; it is the only way to set the prisoner free; the prisoner that is you!

Learn to become the most thankful person. Thank God for every little thing and you will be amazed at the power this one practice can make. There is so much power in being grateful for everything you have. Start really being thankful every day and you will transform your life into having more to be thankful for. It's the law of reciprocity; you get back what you give out. The more thankful you are for the things in your life, the more you will find in your life to be thankful for.

The greatest gift we all have is the gift of Love. It is, by far, our most important gift. Without it, we have nothing. It is Our Lord's supreme command as stated in John 13:34 "A new command I give you: Love one another. As I have loved you, so you must love one another." It is the one thing that is completely renewable, it never fails, it never gives up and it never runs out. Share all the love you have in your heart and you will be restored in full abundance.

The first thirty years of my life are what saturate these pages. You will be pleasantly surprised to find what the next fifteen have held in store for me. I encourage you to pull out the wedges that separate you from your happiness. Trust in your ability to make good choices. Sometimes, we just need to realize that we are smart enough to lead our own lives and not be influenced by negative forces around us.

God is the one voice that counts, the one whose instruction is all you need. Let my life be the proof of His love and divine intervention. When I couldn't see my way through the darkness, He illuminated my path...I am learning to be the light. I hope that you make the realization, that you too can Be something even when you've come from Nothing.

Chapter 11

Pulling out the Wedges

Well, as the saying goes, "What doesn't kill you makes you stronger!" I survived through a lot of hurt but finally learned to channel my emotions in a positive direction.

Until I was willing to take a long look in that mirror and be willing to change some of the things about me that were not working very well, I would never attract anything or anyone better than who I currently was. The law of attraction states, "Like attracts like!"

When I decided to go to college and get an education, quit smoking cigarettes, quit smoking pot and drinking beer, I then became much more marketable to a guy like, Neal! As I built strength within myself, I had long realized that the marriage I was in had to cease. I filed for divorce in 2001 just after the 9/11 attacks in New York City.

That was such a tragic event and so many people were suffering, children had no Mom or Dad coming home that evening. Parents lost sons and daughters and my heart was bleeding with hurt for all those victims who lost their lives for no good reason. They will never get the chance for a do-over. They will never get the chance to shine since those terrorists took away their light.

I thought to myself, "How dare I sit here one more minute being miserable in my life!" I continued by reminding myself that I should be thankful that I have a life and get busy making it the best version I can muster up! It was through others' tragic losses that I gained valuable insight into what was most important to me.

When I closed the door to my toxic marriage, another door opened up and Neal walked through it. He was my knight in shining armor. Of course, as we dated, I was looking for the flaws. I knew he had to have something about him that I didn't like or that irritated me. I sort of interviewed his family, friends and colleagues to discreetly reveal any skeletons he might have had in his closet.

But after several months, I couldn't come up with much. He was the epitome of "everything I've ever wanted in a man." He was drop-dead gorgeous in looks, kind, patient, loving, attentive and quite successful, as I later learned. Neal had no children and was 36 years old, a rare find in the newly approached millennium.

A couple of years passed and we were married in January of 2003. Neal is every bit the man today that I fell in love with almost 12 years ago.

I have the most magnificent life and I am thankful for all that I have been blessed with. In 2004, Neal adopted my two sons and took on the role as their father, who they now call Dad. We have all come to realize that even though Neal and the boys do not share the same DNA, Neal is more of a dad to those boys than their biological father ever was or could be. Blood is not what connects people, love does. This was the beginning of our blended family and it just keeps getting better.

Neal never had any of his own children and we were okay with not having any more than the two boys we had. I guess it was mostly me that pushed the envelope a bit and brought up the idea. But, we had a couple of things working against us. I had a tubal ligation at the age of 21 and Neal had a vasectomy in his life before me. We talked about what path we could take and decided to go and speak to an IVF, (in-vitro fertilization) doctor. Within a short while, we believed this was the best choice for us.

By 2005, our miracle son, Jordan, was born. We couldn't stop there, you can't have one without having two...who would he play with? We yearned to have another child. After deliberating over the process and the toll of this birth, at age 35, took on my body, we looked into adoption as an alternative. After all, we both had a lot of love in our hearts and room in our home to offer a less fortunate child a better way of life. For nearly 11 months, we jumped through all the hoops that the adoption process required of us.

In 2009, Jacob was adopted and came home from St. Petersburg, Russia. Our second generation of children, as we refer to them, has become an incredible addition to our family dynamic. So yes, we have a very blended family but it is the most functional, loving and magical place that these boys could ask for. I praise God for all the blessings and gifts in our lives.

Who would have ever believed that little Heidi Gauthier, from 938 Lisbon Street, would be living the life I am today? I am drug-free, alcohol-free, married to the man of my dreams with four beautiful, handsome boys and basking in the life that I have chosen for myself. I have a degree from college. I have bought homes, sold homes, moved out-of-state, went through in-vitro fertilization, birthed a child, adopted a child, built my dream home of more than 7000+ square feet and vacationed in some of the most fantastic places that most people only ever read about.

I went on to fall in love with the sport of bodybuilding upon entering my 40s. I trained and competed for three years as a natural bodybuilder winning my professional title as an NGA Pro Figure Athlete at age 43. If anyone had told me that this would be my life today, I would have bet against it.

I am proud of myself for recognizing that I am the one who is making the decisions for me and what I want. For years, what I wanted didn't seem to matter much; it was more about everyone else and seeing that they got what filled them up and I would just settle for whatever was left over.

If you want to begin doing some of the things I am doing, start taking control of your life by managing your thoughts and understanding that YOU are worth listening to. What YOU think does matter!

As I have, you must learn to let go of who you were and embrace who you want to become. Is it scary? Is it unfamiliar? Yes! But ask yourself, "Am I ready to take the long, hard look at myself and my life and determine whether I am 'good' with the way things are or not?"

If you are not entirely happy with where your life is at in the present moment, I encourage you to try a different way since yours may not be working optimally for you. Here are a few techniques I have used over the years to really turn my life around.

1) Take Responsibility – I became willing to acknowledge and take ownership of the life I have chosen for myself. My mantra is that...I am where I am as a result of my choices, both good and bad. Dr. Phil says, "You can't change what you won't

acknowledge!" When I decided to take responsibility for my current state of happiness, I simultaneously took control of my future state as well. Everything starts with the decisions we make today which, in turn, spill over into the consequences that create our tomorrow.

2) Reflect – As I reflected back over my life, I saw some things about me that were less than attractive. It wasn't until I was willing to see myself from this objective viewpoint that I could recognize the flaws and defects that had to change if I were to live a different life than the one I was living. Albert Einstein offers us, "You can't solve a problem with the same mind that created it!" As I became willing to call a spade a spade, I realized there were lessons that came from where I had been that were hinting to the direction I was to move in. Look at your strengths and at your weaknesses, there are gifts in both.

3) Acceptance – It is...what it is and/or it was...what it was. I stopped trying to fight this. It is all about the movement of letting go and moving on. I have learned not to restrict myself but allow free mobility of all my being to experience and perceive through the three conduits which I accept information and incoming data...body,

mind and spirit. This is the first step to what is possible next.

4) Forgiveness – Let go of the feelings that bind you and keep you imprisoned in a world of unforgiving. This is the key to a life filled with peace and harmony.

5) Remove & Replace – Take away and discard the pieces that don't "fit" in your new life of happiness, pleasure and abundance. Changing your old habits and unwanted behavior is hard work. For everything you take away that is not working for you, be ready to replace it with something that moves you toward your new objective.

6) Gratitude – Be thankful for everything you have. The more thankful you are for the things in your life, the more things you will have in your life to be thankful for.

This is where the rubber meets the road. I went on to make several changes that amounted to some pretty great successes.

Applying the principles above can help you in changing some things in your life that you are not willing to live with anymore. For example, when I decided to quit smoking, I learned to change my environment. I went from what was comfortable and familiar to what was not. In an effort to break this pattern, I began sitting in a different chair, in a completely different room, drinking juice from a glass, instead of coffee from a mug and I deleted the newspaper from my morning ritual and replaced it with making a list of all the things I wanted to accomplish throughout my day.

I applied this same concept to drugs and alcohol. I no longer "hung out" in bad neighborhoods. When you are the alcoholic who is trying to recover, the local bar cannot be your playground of choice. You will set yourself up to fail.

Break the pattern, as I have, by placing yourself in environments that enhance your ability to thrive and make good choices. I once heard, "If you want to fly with eagles, you've got to stop running around with the turkeys!" Bottom line is this: Environment drives Behavior! If you are trying to stick to a weight loss program, do not hang out at the local buffet. Don't put yourself in an environment that increases your chances of failure; rather look for those that foster your ideal self.

I began looking to increase my level of education so I started visiting the community college in my city. I began talking with the people who could make my dream a reality. Walking those halls and being surrounded by students, teachers and all the educational eye candy that peppered the walls, served as an inspiration for me to continue in this direction. The more

I embedded myself into the fabric of people who were doing what I wanted to do, the easier it became to be pulled along by their current and influenced by their behavior.

I have taken responsibility for my life by choosing what I wanted to see differently. Reflecting back and seeing the person I was has served as an example of what I no longer wanted to be. Learning to accept where I was and where I had been became a first step to deciding where I was going. In repenting for my sins, I have discovered one of the most freeing elements in this whole process, Forgiveness. Jesus went to the cross for us; he was crucified and died for our sins so that we may have eternal life. Many people mistreated him along the way but rather than harboring anger towards them, He instead pleaded to The Almighty, "Forgive them Father, for they know not what they do." If Jesus can forgive us, than I can forgive myself and also those who have hurt me. By giving my wrongdoers the benefit of the doubt, I will hold steadfast to walk in the light of our Lord and forgive those that trespass against me.

We all have wedges that keep us apart from our goals, dreams and whatever the things are that we want most in our lives. When I made the conscious decision to remove unfavorable things in my life, I knew I had to replace the loss of what no longer worked for me with things that brought me joy. Those things that were no longer useful, didn't work or didn't correspond to happiness for me, I quickly replaced with positive ingredients that manifested the results I was looking for.

Our thoughts place us on the path to bring about what we think about. I have spent a lot of time thinking about the kind of life I would like to be enjoying. My thoughts that I have held in my mind have produced after their kind. You can create a shift within your life if you remain clear in your thoughts and what it is that you want most in your life.

Simply stated, "As within, So without," which means whatever you are able to hold consistently in your mind will become your reality.

It is bittersweet as I put the finishing touches on this work that I hope you find inspiring and motivational. I leave you with words that I used to read to myself in the mirror quite often.

As I stood there with tears streaming down my face, gazing at my blotchy, red skin and runny nose, it was all I could do to take control of my childlike hesitant breathing. You know the kind that makes it hard for you to talk, the one that interrupts the middle of your words, and I would proceed to read...

When things go wrong as they sometimes will,

When the road you're trudging seems all uphill,

When funds are low and the debts are high,

And you want to smile, but you have to sigh.

When care is pressing you down a bit.

Rest, if you must, but don't you quit.

Life is strange with its twists and turns

As every one of us sometimes learns.

And many a failure turns about

When he might have won had he stuck it out:

Don't give up though the pace seems slow –

You may succeed with another blow.

Success is failure turned inside out –

The silver tint of the clouds of doubt.

And you never can tell how close you are

It may be near when it seems so far:

So stick to the fight when you're hardest hit

It's when things seem worst that you MUST NOT QUIT!

-Anonymous Author

145

Without a doubt, you will struggle on your way to greatness. As Miley Cyrus sang, "It's all about the climb." Every step counts for something, no matter how big or how small. I have read and reread this poem in an effort to provide me the strength I needed as I encountered many dark times throughout my life.

I always like to reflect on my husband's encouraging words. Neal has said to me many times before, "It's not about how many challenges you've had, but rather, how you've overcome each and every one!" I am living proof that you can Be, Have or Do anything you set your mind to.

I encourage you to pull out the wedges in your life that keep you stuck between where you are and where you want to be. Let go of faulty programming from your upbringing. Employ a refuse-to-lose attitude, where failure is just simply not an option. Believe in yourself!

I leave you with the inspiring words of Audrey Hepburn, "Nothing is impossible, the word itself says, I'm possible!!"

Author's Biography

Heidi S. Quimby is the author of *The Wedge Between Us*. She has written a story about her life and the struggles she has encountered. Growing up in a dysfunctional family did not give her the best chance to be the successful individual she has turned out to be. Heidi has filled the early pages of her book with stories of the hardships, challenges and grief that she has endured. She has written a remarkable story that focuses on overcoming obstacles, never giving up and finding out how to believe in yourself.

By shifting her thinking and opening up to a higher power, Heidi has moved on to create the harmony and bliss that exists in her life today. She has an inspiring, motivational story that will pull at your heartstrings. While possessing a determined and committed aura about her that is both captivating and magnetic, she truly draws people and circumstances to her through her gifts. She is a woman of incredible mental strength, depth and an endless capacity for what is possible next!

Heidi lives in the small town of Perkiomenville, Pennsylvania with her adored husband, Neal. She is the proud mother of four boys, Travis, Luke, Jordan and Jacob. When she is not busy composing, she enjoys the hectic life of a soccer mom, listening to both Christian and country music and is an avid reader. She has also established herself within the bodybuilding arena, earning her professional title in May of 2013 as an NGA Pro Figure Athlete. She attributes her success to maintaining a balance in her life of Mind, Body & Spirit. She can be contacted at Pean5@aol.com.